Behind Her Brand:
Direct Sales Edition

Compiled by Teresa Garrison

Co-authored by:

Elizabeth Campbell Boyd
Lyn Conway
Kari Driskell
Julie Anne Jones
Desiree Wolfe
Lyndsey Baigent
Deb Bixler
Monica Ramos
Karen Clark
Teresa Garrison

Behind Her Brand: Direct Sales Edition
1. Business 2. Marketing

ISBN-10: 069259454X
ISBN-13: 978-0692594544
BUSINESS & ECONOMICS: Entrepreneurship

DEDICATION

This book is dedicated to the Direct Sales Leaders who have let us be a part of their business journey and their personal growth. We appreciate their willingness to take us along for the ride in their pursuit of leading with integrity. We thank them for what they have taught us along the way and we are grateful that many of these introductions have blossomed into treasured friendships.

TABLE OF CONTENTS

ELIZABETH CAMPBELL BOYD
DMC International

Tell us a little about yourself and how you were first introduced to the direct sales industry?

One of my first jobs out of college was working at a hotel. I was contemplating if I wanted to go straight into teaching, which is what I had focused on in college, and decided to take a job at a beautiful resort in the meantime. It was almost immediate, this new found and completely unexpected love for the meeting and travel industry. I don't know if it was the people, the constantly changing schedule, the unplanned hurdles or the fast pace of the day-to-day operations but I knew I had found what I wanted to do.

During this time one of my regular clients was Discovery Toys. It was through this relationship and getting to know Lane Nemeth, Discovery Toys founder, and the company's Diamond Sales Directors that I was first really introduced to the direct sales industry. My relationship with Discovery Toys grew over the years, as I worked with the company on its hotel accommodations, airport transfers, dinner reservations, and spa appointments. I came to know not only the executive staff but also began to build relationships with some of the top producers, and many of these relationships continue to this day.

I remember being impressed and in awe of these women and that infatuation just grew as I learned more about what they did and how they earned their money. The industry provided an incredible opportunity to women in particular. These successful women were enchanting, and so supportive of one another, and I always looked forward to their arrivals. I was especially drawn to how much they wanted others to experience the lifestyle they had created for themselves. It went far beyond recruiting. They wanted others to know there were options to the traditional job scenario and that it was paired with incredible freedom.

Lane Nemeth was so passionate about not only her company but the direct sales industry and what was possible within it. Her enthusiasm was contagious. Eventually I was hired by Discovery Toys, I started working at the corporate office in the meetings department and ultimately was promoted to director of that group.

I don't recall having any specific knowledge of the industry prior to my introduction to Lane and working with Discovery Toys other than of course hearing about Avon and Mary Kay. I was aware of those companies, but I didn't really know or understand the sales model, nor did I purchase products from them. Since then my interest and involvement with direct sales companies has grown and without a doubt led to some of the most impactful relationships of my life.

Share with us what your business is and why you focus on supporting the direct sales industry?

I assist clients with their contractual and logistical needs for their meetings, conventions and incentive trips. Since leaving the hotel industry I have been immersed, by choice, in the direct sales industry. I find it challenging, rewarding and ever-changing. It's invigorating to work with corporate offices to create events that engage and support field representatives. Additionally, I think I have one of the best views of the industry.

I play a role in making sure the corporate vision unfolds as planned, but additionally I get to witness my client's sales force in all stages of creating their own destiny. It is amazing. Watching first-time event attendees, those newest to the company, and often new to the industry, personally grow and be recognized for achievements they didn't even envision were possible is to witness the American dream being realized. I get to hear first-hand stories of being debt-free, of first homes being purchased, of college educations being paid for in cash. I get to be with them when they first taste pasta in Italy, see a waltz in Vienna, or sip a daiquiri on a tropical shore at sunset. It is nothing short of magical and has not only captured my attention but held it for the past 20 years.

What is your favorite thing about the direct sales industry?

Every aspect of it is personalized - each company, each product, each field member and each experience. There is no one way of doing things, from my view. Anyone can be successful with imagination, passion and drive. This is true both for the corporate offices but more specifically for the field leaders. Direct sales companies have internal strategic measurements they use to define success, be it sales volume, recruiting stats, or product margins. And the sales force has countless ways to define what success means, which varies by person.

You can be successful having a hobby, using products at a discount, bringing in some extra cash when needed, building a career or creating a family business. Most of this can be done on one's own schedule. That's what really makes this industry stand out. You set the hours you want to work. The effort put in directly affects the rewards, and I can't think of any other industry where a sales force has that much direct control over outcomes or goals reached. It is the most ingenious model and truly allows people to create, within their own parameters, their own destinies.

What is the most rewarding aspect of working with direct sales entrepreneurs?

Meeting first-time convention attendees just getting started brings me the most joy. Often they don't consider this new venture as a business, let alone that it is their business. They are the CEO. They will get to determine their own path and success. Having a front-row seat to watch them blossom, to see them cross the stage and be recognized for achievements they didn't realize were attainable, to eventually welcoming them on their company's incentive trip – this is pure bliss to me. It's inspiring to witness such endless possibilities. If I am lucky enough, I get to be in the room when you see that spark lit, that a-ha moment take hold. There is nothing like it. That moment is absolutely priceless to me. I think about these field members as I work with corporate clients to shape the perfect experiences onsite during annual conventions and hard-earned incentive trips.

What is your definition of a successful direct sales entrepreneur?

This is the coolest thing about the direct sales industry. From my view, there are as many illustrations of a successful direct sales entrepreneur as there are people representing the direct sales industry. There is something about taking that first step and signing an agreement, then opening the starter kit and diving in with that all-or-nothing attitude. Many are so outside their comfort zone when leading their first party, asking for future hostesses or asking others to join them. Each step taken is a milestone in creating a successful entrepreneur.

I believe being a successful direct sales entrepreneur is an ever-evolving practice. At its base is the confidence to take a leap of faith into a new venture and own it. It can be quite simple. They are successful entrepreneurs if goals are reached. That's another wonderful aspect of this industry; within each company there are guidelines that determine success of one person against another, but the most important measurement is if one's personal goals or needs are being achieved. If so, success has been attained.

What do you consider great characteristics of successful entrepreneurs?

It starts with the definition of an entrepreneur. It's a risk-taker, someone willing to work for something they are confident will bring them the outcome they desire. Someone with initiative. Sometimes this initiative is driven by the need for income; or the desire for something all their own. It requires flexibility to juggle multiple obligations and put in the necessary work.

You have to be motivated and disciplined to make sure you are working in a smart manner to manifest what you most desire or need. Having a clear vision is critical and it is mandatory to set goals or put measurements in place to determine if you are on track. If you get off track, you have to have the wisdom to make adjustments.

An entrepreneur can't be afraid of failure but rather invigorated by it, using the lesson to drive them further on their path of success. But most importantly I think an entrepreneur needs to know their limits and when to ask for help. They need to have the confidence to reach out to those that are achieving what they desire to and ask for guidance. A successful entrepreneur will not allow ego to get in the way of hitting goals.

Some people naturally possess these characteristics, but I believe they can also be learned. Anyone can be a successful entrepreneur, but you have to want it enough to work for it. Gaining an advantage means training for the necessary skill set, to educate oneself by studying those that have already achieved what they are shooting for, listening to constructive criticism and acting on the smart advice of others.

What are your insights about the direct selling industry that will best help people build a strong business?

From my view you have to have a strong reason that you chose your company and your product that makes it personal to you. To be successful you have to believe in what you are representing. You must believe in the company and its mission, the product, or the opportunity and the income. Like anything worthwhile you need to put in the effort and work to achieve goals you set for yourself.

Does any product really sell itself? It seems to me the direct sales industry, like the travel industry, is ultimately a business of relationships. Customers and team members are buying you, your expertise, your excitement, your product, just as my clients are buying me as much as my services. This means you have to not only take the time to get to know your customers or your team but you have to continue to be interested and engaged long after the first order is placed or the recruiting form is signed.

When people speak about direct sales products, I'm fascinated that the focus is often more about their contact or representative from whom they order the product than the actual benefits of the product itself. This is clearly a social industry; it brings people, friends, families and in some instances communities together. I know it is true for me and I hear it time and time again: People place orders with those whom they feel connected. If a person representing a product is not invested or doesn't show any interest in me, future orders simply are not placed no matter how much I believe in the product. To build a strong business you have to acknowledge it is as much about the shopping experience and the representative's commitment in you as is it about the product itself.

What advice would you give someone who is ready to take their business to the next level?

When someone is first recruited, it is all about them, what they want, what they need to do to get started, and what their goals are. But ultimately, the most successful direct sales entrepreneurs have an innate drive toward their own success equal to the desire to assist others to succeed. This is one of the elements that most fascinated me about this industry. It is a community of sorts. The ones I see achieving the most are those who instinctively (be it out of excitement or fear) bring others along for the ride from the beginning.

I have seen many people achieve great things through their own efforts in both sales and recruiting. However, to really explode one's business to the next level it is about your team and the success of those you have asked to join you. This leap is sometimes a shaky one, especially if you have been focused on your own goals and achievements, without consideration of others also wanting what you are shooting for.

This struggle is real, and it can be not only disappointing but also debilitating. I have seen some people, facing an ominous crossroads, navigate through complications with ease and grace after engaging with a trusted mentor or trainer. Sometimes a mentor can be found within the field or corporate organization, and other times it is a keynote speaker from a corporate convention or someone who has been recommended to you. Those who are genuinely open to engage and learn from a mentor or trainer and also execute what is being taught without question are going to grow their businesses. Those who trust the process are the ones who seem the most effective.

What is the best description of the relationship between a field member and their corporate office?

This is an area that can cause much confusion. Vaguely defined gray areas can lead to hurt feelings and resentment. Corporate offices want to work with top leaders to be sure their needs are heard and addressed, and therefore often create environments where ideas and concepts are shared, discussed and acted upon. I have been witness to top leaders who count on being at the table. when new policies or promotions are created.

Confusion can arise when clear operating guidelines are not established. When one side of this relationship has a distinct view on the involvement level, that is left to be assumed by the other side. Therefore, a disconnect puts unnecessary strain on the partnership, especially when things get personal and respect is questioned.

Collaborations work beautifully when a clear set of parameters and expectations are defined and adhered to. It is a huge challenge to reconcile once elements of distrust or favoritism comes into play. Additionally, I have seen many direct sales corporate offices make some tough decisions that are harshly received by the field even though the decisions were necessary to support the overall financial health of the company. When there is trust and transparency, the alliance stays intact and hurdles can be cleared. Like within any business structure, the relationship should be a cohesive one if the members have an understanding of the process and where each participant's realm of responsibility and involvement lays.

Consistency and reproducible are terms often used by direct sales leaders. What are some of the most successful systems you have seen used by top leaders?

One of the practices I have seen consistently used by top leaders is recognition of their team members. The most successful ones recognize all, not just the top performers. The leaders who work to ensure everyone feels they have accomplished something impactful seem to have the most unified and supportive teams.

I first saw this while working for Discovery Toys. I was lucky enough to work for Janice Mazibrook when she was the Vice

President of Sales. Janice would review and study performance reports until she could recognize each leader for being at the top for something. Any behavior would work as long as she was able to recognize them. Top in recruiting and top in selling are the most obvious, but then she got creative and had some morale-boosting fun. First to book a party in a particular month. First in with an order, or an order over a certain dollar amount. I have seen leaders recognize a team member for being the first to sell a particular product in a month, or first to sell 20 of a particular product in a month.

When I see leaders who are consistent in recognizing successful behavior, I see their team mirroring that with their downlines. Recognition becomes your team culture when a system is set up to realize how important praise is, even if it is just listing names or having people stand at team meetings. Then at annual conventions and on the incentive trip everyone is genuinely supportive and celebratory about each and every achievement recognized, not only within their teams but more importantly throughout the entire field population.

What are some of the big AH-HAs you have seen entrepreneurs experience that then propel them to the next level?

From my perspective it has to do with when someone is focused on becoming a leader and the light bulb suddenly goes on. It's when they realize that rising to the top has less to do with their goals and more about the goals of their top team members. When you are recruited the focus is on you, your needs and your goals. That is when the attitude switch needs to take place. To transition successfully to a leadership role your thinking has to shift from your needs and your goals to the team's needs and the team's goals. For many this is a rocky transition. It takes refocusing on where you put your energy and how you approach your business. But when someone suddenly gets it, the transformation is incredible and the momentum and pace at which they move forward is inspiring. Once they get it, they really get it.

What have direct selling entrepreneurs shared with you that they wish they had known when they started?

I have heard many observations over the years, but it has always amazed me that I have heard one thing over and over again. That is the value of not only knowing their own "why" but the "why" of their team members. There might be lots of reasons: adult time away from the house, additional income, the interest to earn a paid vacation for their spouse, the stage recognition. Knowing the "why" of team members is what has had the most impact on their success. Unless one asks and assists their team in getting their needs met, reaching personal goals is much harder if not impossible.

What is a characteristic that you have seen that makes you immediately recognize a future leader?

They come in all shapes and sizes. From my perspective, there is not a single characteristic of a leader or even a short list of characteristics for that matter. You don't have to cook to successfully sell cookware, though it would be considered helpful. Fellow contributor, Teresa Garrison, was an incredibly successful field leader with Discovery Toys, and at the time she did not have children.

I believe true leaders are those who make the most of their opportunities. Some may be shy while others are gregarious. Some may love to speak to an audience while fellow leaders prefer not to ever do so. Leaders are detail-oriented as often as they are unorganized. But those who are genuinely encouraging and thrilled for others' achievements – especially outside their own teams – are the ones I recognize as being able to accomplish all they set out to do. Those who honestly care about others and support their achievements always seem to be the most respected leaders.

What are the mistakes you have seen leaders make that stifle the growth of their teams?

This is an easy one. When I see a leader speaking negatively about the company, it poisons their team more than anything else I have witnessed. It doesn't seem to matter if they are speaking negatively about staff at the corporate office, sharing frustration with their teams about policies or procedures that are either facing some internal changes or system upgrades, or complaining about product or price points. Frankly, I have seen personal riffs that don't get repaired when someone speaks poorly about other leaders or teammates.

Words are precious. Hurtful comments carry a lot of weight and are not easily forgotten. This industry seems to draw people looking for something more; a better way of life, a chance at financial freedom, and a social network. Once a sparkle that originally attracted them is tarnished it is hard for them to recover.

People have enough of a challenge handling hardships in their personal lives and negativity can stifle growth or momentum when it is interjected into their business lives.

What are the biggest surprises/hurdles entrepreneurs face once they become leaders?

Added responsibilities mean a shift in their workload or their focus. Instead of concentrating on booking their personal calendars, their own sales goals and keeping up with their monthly recruiting initiatives; they are now required to lead a team. Often they tell me they were not prepared for the time it takes to nurture a team, to keep them motivated, to communicate to them and to train them. For example, they have to keep their team informed when new promotions or product lines are released.

This is why, from my view, training leaders is so imperative. There is a lot to learn about being in the field that is produced from the corporate offices; through fast start programs and initial communications. However, once you are leading a team, the needs change and vary from team to team. It is a struggle to get the personal direction on what your team needs. When a field member previously attends an annual convention, there is time to focus on their own training and getting their needs met. However, leaders know that a convention becomes more about their team, helping them navigate the various seminar topics, making them feel valued and recognized. In many cases that leader is tapped by the corporate office to participate as a facilitator or trainer in the seminar sessions. They used to attend those events for inspiration and motivation, but now it's where they go to inspire and motivate.

That leaves some leaders feeling the need to grow and learn elsewhere to make sure they stay motivated and fed.

What is the best investment you have seen direct sales entrepreneurs make in themselves?

There has to be a persistence to get involved and keep learning. I recommend attending all company-sponsored events; trainings, conferences, and earn all possible promotions, most specifically the incentive trip. The key to having a successful work experience is investing the time together as a community, networking, sharing, being inspired and inspiring others. Those who take the extra step to further invest in themselves with outside training or mentorship programs seem to have additional confidence. I have seen teams learn from that behavior. If they see their up-line attending company-sponsored events, it sets the expectation that everyone should do so. When leaders share trainings or quote trainers it also sends an equally strong message that constant education is a tool to being successful.

What have you learned about yourself while working with top leaders in the direct sales industry?

What brings me the greatest joy is supporting others in reaching their dreams. It is an amazing feeling to be able to watch someone set a goal, work toward it, sometimes stumbling, but getting up and continuing on, and then experiencing the sweet success of attaining it. It fills my cup to watch these leaders so selflessly share, promote and encourage their team members to be all they can be and often reach heights they never dreamed of. I love hearing personal stories from center stage at annual conferences. It's fascinating being backstage as leaders nervously pace, having never publically spoken before, and watching them find their rhythm and pride at the microphone as they share their journey with the audience. It's awesome to be there when they return backstage giddy, shaking, fulfilled and proud. I really can't think of anything I would rather do than be a part of creating moments that celebrate these leaders. and what they have accomplished. My view, from the wings backstage, really is the best seat in the house.

How does your expertise help someone building a direct sales business?

My expertise is a bit different as I am not necessarily related to supporting someone building a direct sales business, but rather I am a partner reinforcing the efforts of the corporate office in supporting their business and its growth. My role is more indirect though still relevant. I work with my corporate partners to ensure that their events have the right blend of training for the field, who are always in different stages of building their businesses. I assist in hiring the most appropriate outside trainers and making sure that the environment is suitable for learning. I also help establish how they will execute recognition, from what behaviors get recognized, how it will happen from standing in place to crossing the stage, and to addressing the audience.

I strive to ensure that the client's incentive trips provide the experiences promised and that each moment is representative of the hard work put forth to achieve the trip. I oversee all the smaller details to ensure that "the trip of a lifetime" is just that, an unforgettable experience that you want to earn each and every year. I am not necessarily on the front line of helping someone build a direct sales business, but I am nearby making sure that what is being done to support those building a direct sales business is in place and impactful.

What are the top 3 things you would recommend, based on your expertise, that accelerates business growth?

First and foremost, it's to attend your company annual training events. Do whatever is necessary to get there, and encourage others to join you. Not only does it provide incredible training and networking opportunities but it really gives you incredible insight to what your company is all about, the mission and the growth plans for the future. Register early, commit to your company and show others your intent.

Second, do whatever you can to earn the annual incentive trip, and earn it for two. Being able to share these trips with someone who means the world to you is an amazingly joyous experience. And, once they have been your guest on your free trip they will become your biggest cheerleader. The impact the trips have on your business is also immeasurable. One of the greatest marketing tools is being able to promote that you are rewarded with a free trip for doing your job well.

The third is to bring people along with you for the ride. This is a community of relationships and what fun it is to be able to work with your family, your college roommate or your best friend. Other industries don't create such opportunities, where you can honestly select who you get to work with. It is a wonderful gift to be able to create something with others you enjoy and respect. From my view all three of these things promote happiness and enjoyment, which propels growth and success.

Continue the Conversation with Elizabeth Campbell Boyd

 A professional corporate planner specializing in successful execution of domestic and international meetings and incentives.

Elizabeth's comprehensive background in servicing clients combined with accumulated knowledge of the travel industry and trends directly related to the Direct Sales industry provides her with a unique ability to meet the needs of clients while working with the restrictions of particular events, venues and destinations. Elizabeth loves what she does and that shines through on every project she manages.

Below are the various ways that you can connect with Elizabeth and learn more about what she has to offer.

- **Website:**
www.dmc-international.com

- **Twitter:**
@elizabethboyd

- **Facebook:**
www.facebook.com/elizabeth.c.boyd.7

LYN CONWAY
Founder, A Fresh Perspective, Inc.

Tell us a little about yourself and how you were first introduced to the direct sales industry?

I've been part of the direct sales profession a L-O-N-G time! BC (before children), I was a tenured schoolteacher in a public school system in the Chicago area. I left teaching when our first child was born. I wanted to stay home with him and felt I was expected to (it was the 1970s!). Three years later, our second child was born. When she was five weeks old, I was invited to a home party. The "home party" was a fairly new concept and this was the first party I'd ever been invited to. I really had to stretch my comfort zone to go because I was incredibly shy and didn't know my neighbors. It was a daytime party and I could bring my kids, so I packed up the diaper bag and walked down the street to the party. I watched the lady conduct her demonstration. She wasn't very good, but people bought products anyway. Not me, I didn't buy, I didn't book; I just watched. Then I overheard her tell the hostess that she had earned $50! That was a fortune in 1975 and I'd been without an income for three years. I waited until everyone was gone and helped her carry her boxes out to the car. At curbside I asked, "Does your company have any jobs available?" She told me to book six parties and when I had them booked to call her and they'd issue me a kit. Then she drove away! (Not much for recruiting technique, but I'd given her no reason to pay attention to me.)

I was sure I knew who my first six bookings would be. However, when I called them they ALL said, "no"... every single one of them! And that included people like my mom, my sister and my best friend. I could have quit at that moment, but I'm a very determined person. After licking my wounds for a while, I called all six back and said, "Someone's inviting you to parties. Who's inviting you? I'm doing this." They gave me names and I called people I hardly knew – a very hard thing for a shy person to do – and I got the bookings. I then called the lady from the party and told her I had six bookings. She told me to come to an all-day Saturday training where I would pick up my kit.

It was years before I realized what a favor those first six people had done for me! If they'd all said, "Yes," they all knew each other. They would have all invited each other and I'd have seen the same people over and over again. This way, I got started with different circles and had the opportunity to reinvent myself because I was with people who didn't know "shy Lyn."

I was terrible in the beginning! I'd come home from every party in tears. My sweet husband would ask me what was the matter and I'd tell him what a bad job I'd done. He would ask, "Did you do anything right?" I'd think about it and tell him something I had done right and he'd respond, "Well, do that again next time and see if you do one more thing right." We didn't know it then, but my husband was actually my first coach.

Share with us what your business is and why you focus on supporting the direct sales industry?

A Fresh Perspective offers training and coaching to entrepreneurs. Our mission is to help people achieve their own vision of success. I love working with people who decide what they want and do whatever it takes to get it. As I reflect back on my start in direct sales, I realize that if I hadn't been told exactly what to do and been trained to do it, I would never have made it through my very rocky beginning. I knew what I wanted, $50 a week so I wouldn't have to put my kids in daycare and go back to teaching school. That was important money for my family and me! By the end of my first year in direct sales, I was earning more money than I had earned teaching school and I was shocked how quickly my income had grown. I was astonished how consistency and determination had paid off! I want other entrepreneurs to experience the support they need to experience success.

I was with three companies that closed. After each of the first two closed, I quickly did my research to find a new home for my team. Many members of my team counted on the income they were earning and I didn't want to abandon them. After the third company closed, I was tired. My front-line leaders were strong and they relocated their people. I decided, "Three strikes and I'm out," so I got out of direct sales. However, I desperately missed the association with "my people." So when I got an invitation to move to the corporate side in a direct sales company, I jumped at the chance. After seven years in Party Plan corporate offices, I missed being self-employed so I started my company, A Fresh Perspective in 1997. Entrepreneurs are a different breed and my mission is to support their efforts and help them grow and navigate the inevitable speed bumps.

What is your favorite thing about the direct sales industry?

My favorite thing about the direct sales profession is there are no barriers to entry. Starting a business doesn't rely on someone's age, education level, where they live or how much money they have. Anyone can get their money together for a kit and can experience success if they are willing to learn and apply basic, proven success strategies, be persistent, consistent in their efforts and be patient! There are no overnight success stories. It's not like posting a music video on YouTube and having it go viral with millions of views in a week. If someone is willing to do the basics and get better at the basics, they CAN create their own success story.

What is the most rewarding aspect of working with direct sales entrepreneurs?

The Law of 80/20 (Pareto's Law) says that 80% of the results come from 20% of the causes. Successful direct sales entrepreneurs are the 20%. They are the ones who get things done! They KNOW they are both the boss and their own best employee. As the boss, they decide what needs to be done and as the employee, they do it. It's not easy to do what needs to be done day in and day out, but successful entrepreneurs do it anyway. They know everyone has challenges and they find a way over, around or through their own challenges. They don't give up.

Recently, I was coaching a young woman who has four children aged six and under. She teaches elementary school and is growing a strong direct sales team. Her vision is to leave her teaching job and be home with her kids. We worked on time blocking so she would have a plan to get everything done. At the end of the conversation, she asked me, "Do you think I can do it?" I responded, "I know you can do it because you believe you can do it!" Playing a role in helping her achieve her dream is why I do what I do.

What is your definition of a successful direct sales entrepreneur?

My definition of a successful entrepreneur is one who is achieving their goals, no matter how large or small those goals may be. They have a compelling WHY for doing what it takes to build their business, they stay in touch with their WHY and they take action. Their efforts are rarely perfect or even perfectly consistent, but they "keep on keeping' on." They don't make excuses or blame others when things don't go well. They know their success is dependent on two things and only two things: their attitude and their action. If they're not getting the results they desire, they look in the mirror to determine if they need an attitude adjustment or if their daily MO (Method of Operation) needs to be tweaked. They know the habits they cultivate that will make or break them.

What do you consider great characteristics of successful entrepreneurs?

They walk the walk and lead from the front. They don't ask others to do anything they're not willing to do. They have unshakable belief in themselves, their opportunity and the product or service they choose to represent. They exhibit self-discipline of both their time and their emotions. They have a determination others don't possess. Its grit born of being consistently persistence. They are problem-solvers. They are always looking to improve not only what's broken but also what could be better. They're resilient. They're willing to "fail forward" so they try things and when something doesn't work, it doesn't keep them down. They just try something else. This ability to "bend without breaking" makes them stronger each time they fail. They have integrity. People know they can trust them. Due to this quality, their people feel safe and because they feel safe, they are more likely to take risks to stretch and grow. They develop thick skin. They know that taking things personally simply gives away their power. All the successful entrepreneurs I have known are both directable and self-directed. I think that's the "Magic Bullet."

What are your insights about the direct selling industry that will best help people build a strong business?

Don't plan on an "overnight success story." It takes time to build a strong business and that requires patience. There is no standing still when you have your own business. You're either moving forward or backwards. "Getting comfortable" always leads to a slow erosion of what you've built.

For people who need instant gratification, the experience of building a direct sales business may be frustrating. The energy you're investing today (in connecting with people, building relationships, booking appointments and offering the business opportunity) usually doesn't pay you TODAY. I suggest that people think of today's activity as making deposits in an "Energy Bank." The energy you're depositing today pays you dividends in the days, weeks and months ahead. The more energy you expend today in income-producing activities, the bigger the "payoff" in the weeks and months ahead. It's like earning compound interest on your bank deposit.

What advice would you give someone who is ready to take their business to the next level?

Look at the NEXT level and DECIDE to do what it takes to get there. It's counter-productive to look three or four levels ahead. Set a goal to achieve the next level, then the next, then the next…one level at a time. Be clear about what it takes to get to the next level and decide on your strategies. Talk to successful people at that level and ask them for ONE piece of advice – something they wish they'd known before they got there. Then once you get to that level, get SOLID there. Learn what you need to learn to be consistent at that level. Then make your plan for the next level – until you're at the top of your pay plan.

What is the best description of the relationship between a field member and their corporate office?

This is such an important question for the independent field person to consider. Field people tend to form attachments to people in the corporate office and vice versa, but the truth is, corporate people come and go. The field leader's business is not dependent on who is sitting in that corporate chair. It's nice to have people in the corporate office who truly care about the field people, but it doesn't change the responsibilities of the field people growing their own businesses.

The corporate office is the supplier. The field people are their most important customers. One of the biggest reasons to join a direct sales company is so that the corporate office takes care of the "icky stuff" such as: product development, inventory control, paying commissions and bonuses, planning major rewards and incentive trips, technology needs, etc. If the entrepreneur had to do all of that, it would take valuable time. Because the corporate office does that stuff, the time can be spent on "people work" instead of "paper work."

In many companies, the corporate office also shines a beacon on the culture and values of the company and promotes the brand to the public. When that happens, it gives the field person a message to rally around. But when it doesn't happen, the leaders create their own culture and give their team members a safe place to achieve their goals.

Consistency and reproducible are terms often used by direct sales leaders. What are some of the most successful systems you have seen used by top leaders?

I LOVE this question! I think it's one of the most important things a direct sales leader needs to wrap their head around. There are two parts to the question: what system does the leader use to schedule her business time so she provides a duplicatable model and what system does the leader use to train and coach her people. Everything the leader does needs to be reproducible or duplicatable. (Duplicatable isn't in the dictionary yet, but I'm sure direct sales people use is so often that it's just a matter of time before spell-check recognizes it!).

Leaders have to examine how they incorporate their business into their life and ask themselves, "Can the person joining my team do what I do? Would they want to?" The leader needs to closely monitor how they appear to their team. If it looks like they are working all the time, no one will want to be like them. To avoid the appearance of working all the time, the leader should establish a work schedule and include it in their outbound voicemail message, their email signature line and their email auto responder. The schedule can change seasonally, monthly or even daily, but the leader should respect the schedule she publishes. If the leader feels the compulsive need to answer every call and text as it comes in during dinner, after business hours, early in the morning, late at night, it makes the team member feel they couldn't possibly duplicate that behavior.

The second part of the question relates to the system the leader uses to train new team members. I believe the leader needs to train them all the same so she can see which ones respond. When the leader does that, she never needs to fault herself if someone doesn't do what she's been taught to do. And when the new team member sponsors someone, the leader should train both of them together and not expect the new person to know how to train her recruit. If the company provides a training system for new people, the leader should use that system. If the leader continually recreates the wheel, her team will never know how to duplicate her activity!

I had a great AH-HA moment about this in a very unlikely place. My family and I were on vacation in Alaska. We spent a night at a B&B in Juneau. The proprietor of the B&B was a musher. I was very curious about the life of a musher, so I asked her to tell us about it. She described how she chose the dogs for the team and how she trained them. After telling us about the lead dogs, wheel dogs and the rest of the pack, I asked, "How do you pick the lead dogs?" She responded, "Oh, I don't pick them. They pick themselves. I train them all the same and the ones who want to lead show me by their behavior." I have never forgotten the feeling I had at that moment! It's exactly what the direct sales leader does to find who is willing to work. Train them all the same and the ones who want to build a business will show you by their behavior.

I was taught another great lesson about being "reproducible" from a top leader of a party plan in the UK. Neil had a big question mark embroidered into the passenger seat of his Jaguar (no kidding!). I asked him why. His answer had a huge impact on how I teach leaders. He said, "If I can see the question mark, I ask myself who should be sitting in that seat shadowing me. If I always have someone learning as I earn, I get twice the value for my effort. And I identify the people who are willing to take the time to become my apprentice so I know coaching them is a good investment of my time." I teach leaders that they don't have to have a question mark embroidered into the passenger seat of their car. A Post It note with a question mark on the dashboard will do and another on their telephone and their computer. If the leader "never walks alone," they get twice the value for the time they spend on business and identify their 20%.

What are some of the big AH-HAs you have seen entrepreneurs experience that then propel them to the next level?

The successful entrepreneurs I have worked with through the years have all come to the realization that they can make excuses or they can make money – not both – so they become excellent problem solvers. They know that their people are watching them, so they model the attitudes and actions they want duplicated. They value the recognition they receive for their efforts, but they get even more excited when their people are recognized. They learn that building "wide and deep" – personally recruiting and teaching their team members to recruit – leads to both income growth and security.

What have direct selling entrepreneurs shared with you that they wish they had known when they started?

Successful direct selling entrepreneurs tell me they wish someone had shared some of the realities of being self-employed as they were getting started – not to discourage them but to prepare them for what they would experience. The most important realities are:

They are going to hear "No" a lot. Hearing "No" won't kill them and if they keep their eye on their WHY, they will learn to accept "No" gracefully and move on.

"No" doesn't necessarily mean "Never." They need a good follow-up system so they are there when the person is ready to say, "Yes."

Building a business for the long term is all about the relationships. The most successful people are the best relationship builders. It's not a sprint…it's a marathon and requires endurance. At some points in the race, you'll feel that "runner's high." At others you'll hit a wall and think you can't go another inch. Both are normal and you have to just keep moving.

What is a characteristic that you have seen that makes you immediately recognize a future leader?

They do what they've been taught to do and ask, "What's next?" They exhibit that self-discipline I mentioned earlier. They discipline their time. They choose when they're going to work and work when they have chosen to work. They share their schedule (on their family calendar, in the signature line of their emails, on their outgoing voicemail message), so the people in their life know when they're available and when they're not. This habit creates boundaries that function like an "invisible fence." People "at work" know what to expect and people "at home" know when they are available. By clearly defining these boundaries, they avoid the guilt that is typical of entrepreneurs who feel they are "working all the time."

They discipline their emotions. They know "pity parties" don't make them much money and are usually very poorly attended. The most successful entrepreneurs are the ones with the shortest recovery time when something doesn't go well. This doesn't mean they don't experience challenges, problems and missteps. It simply means when things don't go as planned, they feel the disappointment and move on. They get their disappointment time down from a month to a week to a day to a couple of hours.

They are problem-solvers. Everyone has challenges. Future leaders look at their life situation and figure out how to fit their business into it. They don't make excuses.

What do you see direct sales leaders do to keep motivated and encouraging of their team when things aren't going right?

The direct sales leaders who keep themselves and their teams motivated when things aren't going right are the ones who realize what is and what is not in their control. They can't control the actions of others, but they can control their own actions. They can't control external events, but they can control their response.

What are the mistakes you have seen leaders make that stifle the growth of their teams?

Leaders have to learn to hold the reins of their team with a light touch. Many leaders have trouble giving up control so they don't delegate as their team members get secure in their skills. Others let go too soon. They think people are competent to train and coach before they are ready.

Some leaders take a promotion and start to "manage." They stop doing the personal business activities – selling and recruiting – that got them there. They forget their people are always watching them and it's rare to find a team member who will do more than they're doing. I remember being on a shuttle bus on the way to McCormick Place when I was a guest speaker at The Pampered Chef's annual conference. I was sitting next to one of the very top PC field leaders. I asked her if she continued to work her personal business. She replied, "Two shows a week and two recruits a month." Then she continued, "My bonus income for one hour is more than I make on my personal sales for the month, but if I stop working, my people will too." Smart leader!

What are the biggest surprises/hurdles entrepreneurs face once they become leaders?

The biggest surprise is that the people who got them there won't keep them there. People and leaders leave, so they must keep recruiting and sorting and developing the willing.

How do successful entrepreneurs create a direct sales business that perpetuates?

Successful entrepreneurs keep walking the walk. They lead from the front in sales, recruiting and developing people. They foster an environment in which people feel safe and appreciated. They notice what their people are experiencing – both their ups and their downs. They recognize the accomplishments and provide a safety net when their people are falling. They also know when to "bless and release" people who don't want to do what it takes to build a business. They know they don't have the strength to drag people across the finish line, so they match efforts with their people.

What is the one key piece of advice you have given to the leaders you coach that has proven the most successful?

My most important piece of advice is to make time in your life for your business. Most successful entrepreneurs already have a busy life when they decide to start their business. Scheduling is critical. Anyone can get good at the basics if they take the time to practice. But no one starts a business in a vacuum. They have to make space/time in their life for their business. I suggest that entrepreneurs plan monthly (the big picture for the upcoming month), weekly (because no two weeks are exactly alike) and daily (including a list of the most important things to do, their appointment schedule and a list of their contacts that day). I also recommend they include the important people in their life in their planning. When those people feel like they are part of the planning process, they will be invested in helping the entrepreneur succeed. This eliminates much of the internal struggle many entrepreneurs experience when they feel like they're letting family and friends down.

What is the best investment you have seen direct sales entrepreneurs make in themselves?

Entrepreneurs have to keep fresh. This means attending events where they can share ideas with like-minded people. They seek out experiences – conferences, webinars, discussions – where they can "sharpen their saw." They read. They learn. They collaborate.

If you were standing in front of 200 new field members who just joined a direct sales company what 3 things would you share?

I consider it a privilege to have had the opportunity to do this many times! I tell these fresh, new entrepreneurs:

1) You just added something new to your life. You have to carve out time for it. Discuss the time you're going to spend with your family and friends so they know and support your plan.

2) Identify your compelling WHY for taking action. If your WHY isn't bigger than what you fear, you'll procrastinate and never REALLY get started.

3) Promise yourself you'll give it a year. No one gets good at building their own business overnight. You'll feel like quitting a hundred times. You WILL have obstacles. Unless you've decided in advance not to quit, you'll decide it's just not worth the effort.

When I'm feeling poetic, I tell my audience that succeeding in business is like succeeding in marriage. Falling in love is the easy part. Staying in love takes work. It's a choice. My husband, Dan, and I have been married for 46 years. At our 25th Anniversary party, our son, Danny, proposed a toast, "To Mom and Dad – for 20 years of happy marriage!" I whispered to him, "25 years, honey." He whispered back, "I said 'happy'." Very perceptive for a 22 year old! The people who stay married a long time know that staying married is a choice to not quit when the going gets tough. The same thing can be said about being an entrepreneur!

What have you learned about yourself while working with top leaders in the direct sales industry?

Working with direct sales leaders makes me grateful every day that I wandered into this profession! I am in awe of the people I have the privilege to work with. They are self-motivated, hard-working, dedicated, and caring people I'm proud to call friends. Sometimes, leaders call or write to thank me. They tell me they have been successful because of what they learned from me. I respectfully tell them they are successful because they took what they learned and ran with it. I teach everyone the same things. The successful people take the lessons and apply them. Their success is the result of their positive attitude and actions. I'm humbled to be part of their journey!

How does your expertise help someone building a direct sales business?

I've done it. All of it. When I got started, I was voted "least likely to succeed." I was a terrible booker. I didn't recruit for six months. I had every reason to quit but I didn't. I went to every meeting. I learned what successful people were doing. I practiced until I got good at it too. I kept reinventing myself until people wanted to do business with me. I didn't quit. I was tenacious when things were tough. As the years have gone by, some things have changed about the direct sales profession and some things have stayed the same. I've kept up with the changes and continue to offer entrepreneurs "a fresh perspective" on how to be as successful as they choose to be.

What are the top 3 things you would recommend, based on your expertise, that accelerates business growth?

The top three things I would recommend are actually simple concepts. However, they're not easy to do. (If they were easy, EVERYONE would be doing them!)

Treat your business like a business. Schedule ENOUGH time; talk to ENOUGH people; book ENOUGH appointments to let the law of averages work for you. When you do ENOUGH, you develop a business posture and you get "street cred." In time, you can look in the mirror and, with a straight face, say, "I'm a business person!"

Always have a BIG WHY. WHYs change, so you always have to look at your current WHY so you have a compelling reason to stay positive and take action.

FAYC: Forget About Yourself Completely. When you stop thinking and worrying about yourself and what others think about you and start thinking about who you can help with your services, your results multiply exponentially.

Continue the Conversation with Lyn Conway

 Lyn Conway founded A Fresh Perspective, Inc. in 1997. Her mission is to help entrepreneurs achieve their vision of success. Lyn is one of the nation's leading experts in direct sales. She is an internationally acclaimed speaker and trainer because her message touches both the mind and the heart. People leave Lyn's seminars prepared to take action.

Lyn makes her home in Warren, Rhode Island, with her husband, Dan. She has two grown children. She has helped people achieve the success they desire by sharing the lessons she learned about balancing family and business. She describes her proudest moment as when she overheard her children saying that she didn't work when they were growing up.

Below are the various ways that you can connect with Lyn and learn more about what she has to offer.

- **Website:**
www.afreshperspective.com

- **Twitter:**
@afplyn

- **Facebook:**
Lyn Conway Business page: A Fresh Perspective

KARI DRISKELL
Founder, DRISKOTECH

Tell us a little about yourself and how you were first introduced to the direct sales industry?

I remember my mom hosting parties when I was a kid. All the ladies would come to the house, and mom would fix some special snacks, it'd be so fun. I watched my sisters participate in direct sales as a way to contribute to their young families for many years. But as an 'educated woman' with a graduate degree, I was that lady who was very skeptical… at first.

At the time that I considered going into direct sales for myself, I was in my fourth year of teaching middle school math, had a 3 month old daughter, and had to quit all my part-time jobs so I could make pick-up and drop-off times at her daycare. The loss in the extra income, plus the daycare fees was going to hurt our family financially. Eric, my husband, is a teacher and coach at a nearby high school, so bringing in extra income was always something we were doing.

I was invited to a jewelry party by my college roommate and dear friend Amanda. I really wasn't planning on going. I didn't have a lot of extra cash, nor did I wear jewelry, plus I had a new baby in tow. However, she made that "reminder call" the night before the party and convinced me to come.

During the party, the rep, Elizabeth, who is now my good friend, passed around a sheet of paper showing how much she made in her last 10 jewelry parties. As a middle school math teacher, the numbers spoke to me. I immediately told Elizabeth that I thought I might want to do what she does. I figured I could *learn* how to wear jewelry to make that kind of extra income!

Elizabeth came to my home a few days later to share how the business worked. Within the week I signed my contract.

Share with us what your business is and why you focus on supporting the direct sales industry?

With DRISKOTECH, I help direct sellers create "video awesomeness." The industry is evolving as we connect with people on social media and video is playing an important and powerful role. Many direct sellers are making videos for their businesses, but you need to look like you know what you're doing. You don't need to invest in all the fancy equipment people *think* they need in order to do awesome videos. A cell phone and a basic computer will work just fine!

I'm very passionate about working with direct sellers. It's what I did for 10-years of my life! Direct sales helped me stay-at-home with my kids. It gave me something for myself. It helped me get out of the house, pay our bills, and keep my sanity. I owe a lot of who I am today because of my time in the direct sales industry, and because of the people who I've met along the way.

I've been there. And with DRISKOTECH, I'm still teaching and I'm working with awesome women in an industry I love; the people industry.

What is your favorite thing about the direct sales industry?

Definitely the people. Being in direct sales is a people business. I loved my customers, hostesses and the people I'd meet while doing my in-home parties and Facebook parties. I loved my team and connecting with these women as they work their businesses to help meet their needs. I loved my extended sisters in the business and the leaders who motivated and inspired me to be better.

There are great people in direct sales. People with big dreams and ambition. People who desire to be better than they were yesterday. These are the type of people I like to hang out with!

What is the most rewarding aspect of working with direct sales entrepreneurs?

Knowing that I'm making such a positive impact on their business, in their online presence, and in their livelihood. I teach direct sellers and small business owners why and how to brand themselves to their business using video. I teach them how to collect awesome footage with the intent to edit; how to edit using free software available on a basic computer; how to maximize time and create a fast, fun, and engaging video; and I teach them how to upload, where and why.

I help them look like they know what they're doing so they're not putting embarrassing videos out to the universe! Getting a "thank you" from one of "my peoples" really makes my day. Sometimes it's statistics from their Facebook page, sometimes they'll tell me how their retail has increased, or they've gotten more future bookings than they could have ever imagined with their new Demonstration Video they're using in their Facebook parties, or it could just be what their customers & hostesses are saying!

I love hearing how they're connecting on a deeper level with their people, and how their hostesses and customers look forward and even ask when their next video is coming out!

Social media plays a *huge* role in our businesses as we connect, build, & strengthen relationships with our hostesses, customers, friends & family. Video is incredibly impactful – increasing reach and engagement. You've really got to be doing it, or you're going to miss out. You've got to evolve with the industry.

I know I'm helping entrepreneurs make a difference in their business. I know that I'm helping them keep things personal and connect with their customers and hostesses while in an online environment. And I find that very fulfilling.

What is your definition of a successful direct sales entrepreneur?

We each get into direct sales for different reasons, don't we? Those reasons are constantly changing as life happens. The key is identifying what your goal or need is, creating an action plan, and continuing to strive for that goal. Re-evaluate at a reasonable time, adjust if necessary, and go at it again. Sometimes we don't reach the end we may be aiming for, but does that mean that we've failed? No. It's about the progress, the journey. Focus on constantly improving yourself. Develop a growth mindset.

What do you consider great characteristics of successful entrepreneurs?

Wow! This is a great question. Great characteristics of a successful entrepreneur would have to be:

- Someone who doesn't back down, who doesn't give up. Someone who can handle adversity because failures and setbacks are part of the process of improving.
- Someone who's willing to be innovative. Someone who isn't easily intimidated or afraid of work.

- Someone who is positive, genuine, truthful, and true to herself. Someone with integrity.
- Someone who can hear a "no" or a "no, thank you" and say to themselves, "no, problem, who's next?"
- Someone who invests in themselves; always learning and developing.
- Someone who puts others first; lifts them up. Someone who's an encourager, who helps others discover who they are, who stretches not only themselves, but others by setting an example.
- Someone who's confident, but humble. Who can laugh at themselves.
- Someone who loves and is passionate about people. And someone who is willing to make a difference in this world.

What are your insights about the direct selling industry that will best help people build a strong business?

I'm going to tell you something you already know; there's a slew of people in direct sales. Not only in direct sales, but in your industry. And since I work in video and editing, I'm going to tell you a little something: you need to be branding yourself and your face to your business to help you stand out from the crowd of other reps.

It'll help you make a name for yourself. People will remember your face, your voice, and your mannerisms. They'll connect you to your business and they'll start to feel like they know you, like you. With the power and influence of social media and so many direct sellers taking their businesses, all or some, online, you've got to be making your own videos. You do not want to be "just another rep." *You* are what makes you different! So you've got to let people in; you've got to show them who you are and a great way to do that is in video.

People can feel the emotion that you share in video; your passion, your love, your excitement, and your humor. Trust me, you're going to be missing out if you're not making videos for your business. It's time to evolve with the industry.

When I was in direct sales, my videos got people talking. Of course, this grew my following and helped grow my online presence in my business. My people would ask when my next video was coming out. They'd look for them. Since the videos were short, fun, fast-paced, and delivered valuable content from their jewelry lady, they'd watch them! Plus, they'd share my videos, which introduced me to *their* online friends and family, which grew my following even more, way more than if I had decided to play small online.

Video helps people decide whether or not to make a purchase. It helps with their understanding of your product or service. Plus, they'd rather watch a video than read the same information! Using video keeps things personal and connects you with your audience on a deeper level. Not to mention, that video is the type of post that typically gives you the highest reach & engagement in social media.

What advice would you give someone who is ready to take their business to the next level?

Get comfortable being uncomfortable. Plan to take risks. Be willing to be bold. Rock the boat a little. And, duh, make videos, making sure to put your face in it. I get it, making videos may seem like a risk in many ways. But if you would be willing to learn how to do it, do it well, and consistently, you'd be surprised at how it would benefit your business.

Consider using edited videos on those high-trafficked promotional videos or your product demonstration videos for your Facebook parties. Edited videos engage your viewer, but also respects and maximizes time for your audience. And you can show and say more in less time!

You don't need any fancy equipment to do it! You can do it all with your cell phone and a basic computer, which is exactly what I use. Remember, you want to look like you know what you're doing when you make a video. You want to be taken as a serious, but fun, business person, because that's exactly what you are.

What is the best description of the relationship between a field member and their corporate office?

A partnership for sure! They totally support each other. Home office supports the field member, and without the field member doing what they do, there'd be no reason for the home office. With that being said, there should be a mutual respect between the two. Reps, hear me out with this. If you have a question or a complaint about something that has happened out in the field and you contact your home office customer service department for guidance, make sure that your attitude is one that's in problem-solving mode, not complaining and "being a jerk to anyone who talks to you about it" mode. Nothing gets solved in that way. I'm sure your home office wants to help you work through whatever question or concern you have. They're there to help.

Consistency and reproducible are terms often used by direct sales leaders. What are some of the most successful systems you have seen used by top leaders?

Having systems helps you focus on more important things like on the people, your hostess, your team, and your family. Especially as leaders, having a system allows you a way to help your team, so they don't have to recreate the wheel! When you decide to hire an assistant to help you having systems in place helps them help you, too.

Hostess coaching systems, an in-home party system, a Facebook party system, a follow-up system, a helping a new rep system, and a training system are all must-have systems that successful leaders have. It's important that you set these systems up earlier rather than later, because at some point you're going to wish you had them in place. Of course, our systems are constantly getting tweaked. The idea is that you don't just "wing" it in your business, otherwise craziness sets in. Ha!

Staying consistent helps you keep your head in the game and keep positive. They say that no activity breeds negativity. By having a consistent business with systems in place, you can be a happy direct seller.

What are some of the big AH-HAs you have seen entrepreneurs experience that then propel them to the next level?

As with ANY business, when you can persevere through a "valley," you'd be amazed where you come out on the other side. It's dark always before the dawn. Good does come out of overcoming obstacles. Remember it's about the journey. Also, remember the importance of branding yourself to your business. You *have to* set yourself apart from the rest. You have to! What sets you apart from everyone else is *you* and that means your face and your personality.

Yes, you can brand yourself by using selfies in social media, but utilizing video helps you connect with your people on a much deeper level. It helps you meet new people through your YouTube channel, through your Facebook fan page, in your Facebook parties, Instagram account and more! People get to see you, *feel* you. However, you have to be willing to put yourself out there, and you have to look like you know what you're doing to be taken seriously.

What have direct selling entrepreneurs shared with you that they wish they had known when they started?

Of course, I hear things like, "I wish that I had shared the business opportunity right out of the gate." Too often, we think that we have to have our feet wet in the business; know the ins and outs of our company, and have so many parties under our belts before we *think* we're qualified enough to start sponsoring other people into our business. That's just not true.

The fact of the matter is; you're being selfish by not sharing the business opportunity with others. How simple is it to say that you can learn together on this journey? Plus, when you're just beginning to embark on such an exciting journey, now's the time to share! Excitement is contagious and you'll want to have your friends along for the ride with you.

Direct sales is an opportunity for women to help meet their needs. Not sharing the opportunity that's good enough for you, is like cutting a piece of the most delicious cake and enjoying it in front of your friends without asking if they'd like a piece.

Another thing that I hear a lot is that they wish they had known earlier the impact that making videos for their business would have on their influence. When you start implementing videos on a regular basis, then you're going to see your reach and engagement on your Facebook page increase. Additionally, the engagement in your Facebook parties will increase. Don't be surprised if you also see your sales and bookings increase, too.

Why? Because you're going to make connections, and build and strengthen relationships! People will be able to see your mannerisms, feel your emotions, smile along with you, and soon feel like you're good friends! You'll be connecting on a deeper level and it will assist you in keeping things personal. Let's face it, we're in a relationship driven business!

What is a characteristic that you have seen that makes you immediately recognize a future leader?

Fiery passion. A passion within for greatness. A desire to excel and to be better than they were yesterday. They want to learn and grow. They have a fiery passion for "more." They love helping. They have a fiery passion for people.

What do you see direct sales leaders do to keep motivated and encouraging of their team when things aren't going right?

They keep things in perspective. They keep their "why" in front of their eyes and are consistently working on their own personal businesses to stay motivated. Plus, they surround themselves with other like-minded individuals who have the same fiery passion for greatness! It's hard... because there's going to come a time when things aren't going your way. With the right perspective, the right attitude, and a positive mindset, a good direct sales leader isn't going to wallow in 'the valley.' They're going to do what needs to be done to put their minds back on track and keep going, one step in front of the other.

What are the mistakes you have seen leaders make that stifle the growth of their teams?

Thinking that they're all that and a bag of chips. Listen, it's not about you. It's never *been* about you. It's about your people, your customers, your hostesses, and your team. If you turn the focus to you, you're going to go stagnant, stale, and then go backwards.

Do you have to brand YOURSELF in your business? Yes. However, you need to build THEM up in the meantime. Train your people. Connect with your people. Build relationships with your people. Encourage them. Inspire them. Motivate them. Set the example.

What are the biggest surprises/hurdles entrepreneurs face once they become leaders?

Themselves.

First there's self-doubt. Especially as women we all suffer from this at some point. There are plenty of people planting seeds of doubts within us, we don't need to help them do it. Separate yourself from these "Negative Nelly's." If you can't write them off, distance yourself when you need to and get your mindset in the right place again.

Secondly, there's the idea that you are all that and a bag of chips. So you loosen the reigns a little and quit developing yourself and/or your people. Or turn the focus to yourself. This is never good, your people will see right through that.

And then, there's the whole organizational piece. When you're a leader, you've got a lot on your plate. It would be easy to get overwhelmed. This is really when systems help a ton, but you've got to have them in place; you've got to prepare yourself to get to this point.

How do successful entrepreneurs create a direct sales business that perpetuates?

By finding time to work a little bit every day, staying in a positive mindset, and by surrounding themselves with other like-minded entrepreneurs.

What is the one key piece of advice you have given to the leaders you coach that has proven the most successful?

Don't be afraid to put yourself in videos and put them on YouTube. I hear a lot from direct sellers about how this has helped them grow their teams, stay connected to their team members, and expand their businesses by increasing their retail and their bookings. By doing videos, it helps with the know, like, and trust factor. People really feel like they get to know you when they watch you in a video. It's an opportunity to be transparent and genuine. They get to feel your passion and your emotions – and emotions are contagious.

Then there's YouTube. YouTube is a powerful tool. Since Google owns YouTube, when someone runs a search, YouTube videos pop up. Bam! When you utilize the description & tags well with public videos, you'll be "found" easier when people run searches for those key words! Plus, when you organize your channel with playlists, your channel can be navigated easily. Adding videos to your business can be a game changer.

What is the best investment you have seen direct sales entrepreneurs make in themselves?

The best investment is to invest in yourself. Direct sellers who are willing, able, and eager to learn and then *implement* what they've learned are the most successful.

Of course, working in video these are the must-have videos I see someone really needing: a trailer, a Facebook party demonstration video, hostess coaching videos, a follow up video, a marketing plan video (to recruit), and the know-how so they can create their own edited videos, like with my self-paced editing courses. Having these things in their systems sets them up for having great success online.

With videos you'll reach more people. Meet more people. Connect with more people. You'll be able to sell to more people, and then be able to bless more hostesses with free product at the same time.

If you were standing in front of 200 new field members who just joined a direct sales company what 3 things would you share?

1. Have fun. If you're going to do anything in life, you should enjoy it. Enjoy your business, your relationships, and enjoy yourself. Not necessarily in that order.
2. Work. Don't be afraid of it. Great things come from work. Work your business, work on your relationships, and work on improving yourself.
3. Be You. Direct sales is not a cookie cutter business. Thank goodness! Be true to you and who you are. Let others love you for who you are. You are meant to bring greatness to the world. Don't sell yourself short. And definitely don't let yourself be "just another rep."

What have you learned about yourself while working with top leaders in the direct sales industry?

I've always known I was fun. I've always known that I could teach. By teaching middle schoolers for 7 years, I knew that I could deliver content in a fun and interesting way. My experience as a rep in the direct sales industry for 10 years taught me that we are no different than those middle school kids. We still want valuable information and prefer it delivered in an entertaining fashion.

What I've learned about *myself* from working with leaders in direct sales through DRISKOTECH is that I've awoken a passion; my "calling," if you will. I have a deep desire to help as many direct sellers as I possibly can be able to stand out from the crowd of reps in their industry, share their passion of people and their product while being true to themselves, being able to share who they are with the world and look like they know what they're doing so that they can be taken seriously.

How does your expertise help someone building a direct sales business?

I teach video & editing. I help direct sellers create video awesomeness as they take all or some of their business online.

You will want to be taken seriously as a business owner. Yes, even in direct sales. You're going to want to look like you know what you're doing and I teach that, using things you already have; a cell phone and a basic computer.

People are utilizing social media for their business like never before and creating their own videos. However, you don't want to put up crappy videos; ones that don't hold the attention of your viewer, ones that don't engage your audience, or ones that don't look like you know what you're doing. If you don't get to the content fast enough, or if you put out a super long video, no one's going to watch. Of course putting up any video is better than no video at all… because at least you're putting yourself out there and getting started.

This is what I teach at DRISKOTECH. I help the direct seller feature themselves, their personality, & their product in social media worthy videos. I have self-paced editing ecourses and video services to help you. Plus, I have a really great free gift on my website to help inspire you with video content to help you connect with your people.

What are the top 3 things you would recommend, based on your expertise, that accelerates business growth?

1. Make videos using the tips I share at DRISKOTECH.
2. Use YouTube to host your videos and make a lot of them.
3. Do not be a pushy sales person. Don't forget to connect with your people on real life terms and topics. They want to get to know you, not just the you who sells this or that. (Tap into my FREE GIFT on my website to help you with video content that includes behind-the-scenes of your life, too!)

Continue the Conversation with Kari Driskell:

 Kari Driskell, from DRISKOTECH, has developed an engaging, fast, and fun style for your online videos. A Masters in Education, 7-years of middle-school teaching, & 10-years in a consistent & successful direct sales business, she can teach you, too, how to create "video awesomeness" using your cell phone & a basic computer. Kari is the mother of two busy girls, excels in run-on sentences, loves Harry Potter, coffee, sweatpants, & believes in keepin' it real.

Below are the various ways that you can connect with Kari and learn more about what she has to offer.

- **Website:**
  www.driskotech.com

- **YouTube:**
  www.youtube.com/driskotech

- **Facebook:**
  www.facebook.com/driskotech

JULIE ANNE JONES
Founder, Julie Anne Jones LLC

Tell us a little about yourself and how you were first introduced to the direct sales industry?

I'm a direct sales corporate consultant, keynote speaker and trainer, an ICF accredited life and business coach, and the CEO of Julie Anne Jones, LLC. I am married to the love of my life John and we live in Walla Walla, Washington. I have two almost-grown sons, Sam and Eli, and two grown step-children, Chad and Chelsey. I have a degree in theatre and love to sing so much that I travel 500 miles round trip every other week to sing with the Pride of Portland Sweet Adelines Chorus, one of the top four choruses in the world.

When I found direct sales, I was a young stay at home mom with two little boys and was seriously stressed around money. I was actually looking for a part time job I could work in the evenings when I found my direct sales business. I was visiting my family in Portland, Oregon and my sister had a jewelry party. I never really even gave joining as a representative a second thought until the consultant called me and explained how much money I could make with his company.

I was skeptical but decided since the investment was low, I might as well give it a try. I was an orphan when I started my business. I didn't have a local upline (the couple who sponsored me lived 4 hours away) and I didn't have any experience. I got the kit in the mail and a copy of the format my upline used to do parties, and basically started from scratch. I didn't really have any training to speak of, and I had to pretty much teach myself the how-to's of direct sales. I got bits and pieces here and there from my upline and company trainings, but I really was flying by the seat of my pants.

I started doing 3 parties per week (because that's what my upline told me to do) and within two months of starting my business, I was number one in the country in my division in personal sales. Honestly, in the first three months of my business, I was succeeding in spite of myself (maybe some of you can relate to that).

Share with us what your business is and why you focus on supporting the direct sales industry?

I'm known for my authentic and easy-to-use scripting and I specialize in specific language and tools for success in direct sales. As a former direct sales professional, I built a party plan business for several years. I consistently held three parties per week and was winning national awards yearly. I also built a national team with a network marketing company using the internet. I'm known as "the systems queen," and can break down just about any concept or big picture problem into doable steps. I teach simple systems that work for anyone.

I believe that systems are crucial for direct sellers. At my first company convention, I walked the stage and took home a stack of awards. Honestly, I didn't even know what I was winning or what half of the awards were for that night. I just kept hearing my name called and running up on stage in a daze. It was all completely overwhelming. I remember sitting in my hotel room after the awards banquet, looking at this stack of awards, and realizing I had absolutely no idea what I had done to get here. Not only that, but realized I certainly didn't know how I was going to teach my small but growing team how to succeed. Plus, my business was taking over my life, causing stress in my family, and I felt like I was always working to keep up. Honestly, it wasn't what I had signed up for.

What I discovered very quickly was that I had to have systems or I was going to fail. I'm a fairly systematic person anyhow, and I became very aware of the fact that the success I experienced, all of the activity and things I had to remember to take care of every week, was beginning to completely derail the balance in my life. I had to do something to manage it or I was going to burn out. So I started creating a very systematic way of operating my business. Those systems are the same systems I teach people today as a direct sales trainer.

What is your favorite thing about the direct sales industry?

When I started my business, as I shared above, I was able to succeed almost in spite of myself. That's how easy direct sales really is. Once you understand that and then add some simple systems for creating your success on purpose, doing it the same way every time, you've got yourself a no brainer business that can literally pay you full time income for a part time investment. This can be done all while working from home, raising your kids, and working your business around your life instead of the other way around. I also love the relationships that form in our industry. They are, in my opinion, almost as valuable as the business aspect of the industry. That's actually two, but I couldn't decide between them so my rebel side took over.

What is the most rewarding aspect of working with direct sales entrepreneurs?

I find entrepreneurs from any industry to be courageous, hard workers, and action takers. It's fun to work with people like that.

Add the element of caring and relationship building that is required from direct sales entrepreneurs and you have, in my opinion, the perfect client!

What is your definition of a successful direct sales entrepreneur?

Someone who has created a business (whether that's one party a month or three parties a week, a small team or a team of thousands) that works for them and that they consistently work and build. A direct sales business really is the perfect business because you can choose to be a hobbyist, part-time rep, or full-time rep, and there's room for success at each and every level.

What do you consider great characteristics of successful entrepreneurs?

They are bold, brave, smart, resilient, flexible, positive, open-minded, and willing to make a commitment and investment into their businesses. They understand that there's no such thing as "easy money" or a "turnkey" business without effort and follow through on their end. The difference between a successful direct seller and one who fails is, in my experience, consistent action and follow through. The more you're willing to work for your success as a direct seller, the more successful you'll become.

What are your insights about the direct selling industry that will best help people build a strong business?

This is a relationship business. I hate it when people say they would love to work in our industry but they aren't good at sales. As a direct seller, you are not in the business of selling anything. Your job is to build relationships, share your passion for your product and your company, and create an experience at your parties for your customers and hosts. If you do that, your products really do "sell themselves" and you'll find yourself with plenty of booking and recruit leads.

What advice would you give someone who is ready to take their business to the next level?

Taking your business to the next level really involves three steps.

1. **Decide where you're going.** You'll miss 100% of the targets you aren't aiming for. So first, decide EXACTLY what you want and when you want it.

2. **Make sure you clearly define what it's going to take for you to get there.** I find my clients often say they want the next level of their compensation plan (for example), but when I ask them exactly what that will take, they have no idea. So make sure you know how many team members, leaders, etc. it will take for you to get to the next level.

3. **Reverse engineer those numbers to make sure you'll hit your goal.** If you need two new team members each month for three months, how many recruiting interviews will you need to do a month to get two people to say yes? Where will you find those people to interview? How many parties will it take to get at least ten recruiting interviews? You get the idea.

What is the best description of the relationship between a field member and their corporate office?

First and foremost, remember that you are an independent consultant and you are responsible for your own success. That being said, you also have voluntarily signed a contract with your home office to abide by their rules and to allow them to define (and change in the future) your compensation plan and team structure. This is a tricky relationship, and in my experience, the only constant is change when it comes to your corporate office. They don't change things just to shake things up and upset people. They do it for a myriad of reasons, most of which have to do with helping you succeed.

There is a lot you have no control over when it comes to your relationship with your corporate office. So being very clear about that going in and not fighting against it or complaining when things change is part of your job. That being said, it's also completely within your rights (and your responsibility) to communicate your challenges and frustrations to your corporate office in a way that's fair and appropriate. That may mean working through your upline. Make sure you understand the structure for airing grievances and resolving conflict. Then stick to that structure when you're in this process.

Consistency and reproducible are terms often used by direct sales leaders. What are some of the most successful systems you have seen used by top leaders?

Most of the leaders in our industry didn't set out to be leaders. They found this thing called "direct sales," decided to give it a try, started to have some success, and before they knew it, were leading others without really being trained or prepared. The leaders

I coach generally come to me with virtually no systems in place and drowning because of it. They've often times experienced fast growth and their lives are spinning out of control with no balance whatsoever around their business or teams. So having systems in place for:

- **Your schedule** (when you work and when you DON'T)

- **How you work with your team** (including training new representatives, supporting and training leaders, and education for your entire group)

- **Your own personal business** (including host coaching, customer support, and your own parties)

- **And the administrative side of your business** (including managing your online business, social media platforms, budgets, banking, and taxes)

All are crucial to maintaining the harmony in your own life. Remember, you most likely started this business because you wanted to be more present for your kids and/or family, and not because you wanted to succeed at the expense of them.

What are some of the big AH-HAs you have seen entrepreneurs experience that then propel them to the next level?

The biggest ones, in my opinion, are those that happen when someone attends their first live national conference. They have a chance to learn from guest speakers and the best in the company and to see women just like themselves walking the stage, being recognized for their accomplishments, and earning huge paychecks. I tell my clients, if you can get someone to a national conference, they'll most likely go home and fly!

What have direct selling entrepreneurs shared with you that they wish they had known when they started?

How to share the passion they felt for their products and company in a way that gets people excited (and kept them from feeling "pushy"). If you can tap into this early on, it makes virtually everything easier.

What is a characteristic that you have seen that makes you immediately recognize a future leader?

People who are goal-oriented, driven to succeed, and who consistently set goals make the best leaders. They don't let obstacles stop them (even if they slow them down) and they stay focused on what they want. Those types of people always tend to be positive people by nature, which attracts others to them naturally.

What do you see direct sales leaders do to keep motivated and encouraging of their team when things aren't going right?

They focus on the things they can control and, more importantly, let go of things over which they have no control. I've seen leaders keep their teams motivated through company restructuring, huge changes in compensation plans, and big dips in the economy. The key is to keep asking the questions (of themselves and their teams), *"What can you control and what can you do about what you can control? What action can you take?"*

What are the mistakes you have seen leaders make that stifle the growth of their teams?

I'd say the biggest mistake is the opposite of what I've shared above. Focusing on issues over which they have no control or feeding drama on their team, which they can't solve. The more you focus on a problem, the more power you give it. If you're channeling your focus toward something you can't control, it grows in your immediate experience and causes more and more frustration. Complaining about corporate office changes or the fact that "nobody is booking parties," or even allowing team members to complain and "buying into" what they are saying sabotages you quicker than anything else.

What are the biggest surprises/hurdles entrepreneurs face once they become leaders?

Time management and making sure their business doesn't take over their lives. Most manager-type personalities are also workaholics and it's easy to find yourself working all the time. Especially if you're doing this without systems (which I find most leaders do), your life can spin out of control very quickly.

How do successful entrepreneurs create a direct sales business that perpetuates?

By sharing their passion for their product and their company at every possible turn. Not only is it the easiest way to share, but it makes people want to learn more. Curiosity is also a key component to growth, since asking people questions empowers them to share with you, which gives you opportunities to share your passion with them from a perspective that matters to them. You can only do that if you ask and listen.

What is the one key piece of advice you have given to the leaders you coach that has proven the most successful?

Take the time to figure out what you do that makes you successful and put those practices and principles into duplicatable systems that can be easily done by others. The more systems you have in place, the more successful you'll be. And the more those systems come from what you're already doing, the easier they are to implement and teach. The key is to figure out what you're doing that's bringing you success, tweak those systems, eliminate the things that aren't supporting you, and then teach the resulting systems to your team. It takes a little time but it's totally worth it, both for your own business and as you teach others to be successful.

What is the best investment you have seen direct sales entrepreneurs make in themselves?

Not surprisingly, since I'm a coach, my answer is personal and professional coaching. A coach helps you see yourself and your business through a fresh set of eyes and make specific and powerful changes based on what you have clearly defined that you want out of your business. They also hold you accountable so that you "show up for yourself" on a consistent basis and do what needs to be done to get what you want. I'd say that virtually all of the top leaders in our industry have worked with a coach in their direct sales career (and many consider it an essential investment in their ongoing business).

If you were standing in front of 200 new field members who just joined a direct sales company what 3 things would you share?

1. **Be yourself.** People resonate with you being you. Don't try to be someone else. Find out how you communicate best and make sure you are always coming from that core of authenticity whenever you're showing up in business. Even if you're borrowing ideas from others, make them your own before you try to share them. Say things in your own words and change or tweak the process so that it feels comfortable for you.

2. **Ask more than you tell (and really listen when you ask).** Curiosity is one of the most important traits of successful people, and direct sellers are no exception. When you are curious about someone else, you make them feel valued and they open up to you. This works in every aspect of your business, from booking to recruiting to selling. Just get curious and ask questions. Once you know what's important to someone else (because you've really listened to their answers to your questions), you can share whatever you want to share (from the opportunity to book a party to your business opportunity) from the perspective of why it's important to them.

3. **Follow up.** The fortune is in the follow up, and those who ignore this aspect of their business will not succeed. Period. We are in the business of building relationships and you can't do that without following up. And I'm not talking about just sending a text or hitting the "like" button on one of your customer's Facebook status updates. I'm talking about picking

up the phone (even if you really, really, REALLY don't feel comfortable doing that), connecting with people, and offering service and value to them on a consistent basis.

What have you learned about yourself while working with top leaders in the direct sales industry?

I've learned so much. Mostly, I've learned to be myself and speak and share from the heart. When I'm most authentic, I'm connecting with my clients and that's always the best for both of us. I've also learned that all women are way too hard on themselves, myself included. We all make mistakes and people are much more understanding of those mistakes than we are of ourselves when we make them. Give yourself some grace and let it go.

How does your expertise help someone building a direct sales business?

As I said in the beginning of this interview, my systems grew out of my own experience as an overwhelmed direct seller. I've used the systems I teach and I know they work. I love working with action takers who are passionate about making a plan and then following through with deliberate action. I'm not the perfect coach for everyone because I'm pretty straight forward and I hold my clients accountable when they don't show up and do what they say they're going to do. But that's also what I believe my role is as their coach. We have the agreement up front that I'll kick their butt when they need me to, and for my clients, that works.

What are the top 3 things you would recommend, based on your expertise, that accelerates business growth?

1. **Create at least three specific goals for your business** and put a timeline on when you'll accomplish them. You have to know where you're going before you can get there.

2. **Commit at least a little time every single day to your business,** and go into that time with a clear plan for what you'll accomplish. Even if it's just 20 minutes, if you have a plan, you can accomplish a lot (as long as you shut down email, Facebook, and your cell phone so you can truly focus).

3. **Be patient with yourself and don't get discouraged** when things go wrong. The difference between a successful direct seller and someone who gives up is simply not giving up. Successful direct sellers have the same setbacks and obstacles as those who give up. The difference is, they learn from those setbacks and keep moving forward. So keep going, no matter what. Just don't give up.

Continue the Conversation with Julie Anne Jones:

Julie Anne Jones has been training & coaching direct sellers for the past 10 years through live corporate events and as a popular online trainer. Known as "The Systems Specialist," Julie Anne teaches simple systems for creating a successful direct sales business. She is also known for her authentic and easy-to-use scripting and specific language and tools for success. To learn more about Julie Anne and her products and services, visit her at www.julieannejones.com.

Below are the various ways that you can connect with Julie Anne and learn more about what she has to offer.

- **Website:**
  www.julieannejones.com

- **Twitter:**
  www.twitter.com/julieannejones

- **Facebook:**
  www.facebook.com/julieannejonesinc

DESIREE WOLFE
Business Strategist

Tell us a little about yourself and how you were first introduced to the direct sales industry?

I left the hospitality industry 8 years ago and found myself smack in the middle of an assistant sales position for a successful direct sales company. My experience with direct sales up to that point had only been from growing up in a Tupperware household. My mom sold the products and our cupboards were full of inventory. I had no idea how much the industry would have an impact on me over the following years.

Although I had years of sales and marketing experience I was amazed at the motivation and drive of the inspiring women who had built their own business from one box of products. After I left my corporate position I continued to be involved in the industry. First in a supportive role by assisting leaders with their administrative needs and now as a business strategist.

Share with us what your business is and why you focus on supporting the direct sales industry?

As a Business Success Strategist, I help female entrepreneurs create the right mindset and business strategies so they can take action that is in line with their vision. Supporting the direct sales industry comes naturally for me after spending 6 years in a direct sales corporate office. I have made some amazing connections and have grown a very large network of direct sales connections. I find myself constantly being drawn back into this industry because of the motivation and empowerment.

What is your favorite thing about the direct sales industry?

The direct sales industry provides women (and men) an opportunity to start a business in a way that reduces overwhelm due to support structure you receive. For those that don't feel they can start a business, the direct sales model gives them an option. By giving someone a business in a box they have the chance to follow their dreams of being an entrepreneur and help others build their empires.

What is the most rewarding aspect of working with direct sales entrepreneurs?

The most rewarding aspect of working with direct sales entrepreneurs is the support they are willing to provide each other. Even as large as the industry is, I find very few direct sales professionals who are in competition mode. They are very supportive of the women that are around them. They are ready to empower and uplift not only their team members but members of the industry.

What is your definition of a successful direct sales entrepreneur?

A successful direct sales entrepreneur is extremely supportive of her team and leads by example, no matter how big or small her downline is. She considers her business more than a hobby and treats it like she is the CEO. She seeks business support, training and encourages her team members to do the same. Her business is driven by her passion and determination. Additionally, her business supports her lifestyle.

What do you consider great characteristics of successful entrepreneurs?

I believe there are several common characteristics of successful entrepreneurs:

- **Passion** - You absolutely must love what you do. Successful entrepreneurs are passionate and they believe they can change the world. If you are not truly passionate about your work, you will never be happy with where you are in your business.
- **Vision** - When you are an entrepreneur you see the opportunities around you. Being able to see overlooked niches or unsolved customer problems gives you a step above the competition. By having vision, you allow yourself the ability to dream hard enough so you can really see those dreams becoming reality.
- **Belief** - You MUST believe in yourself, your value, your team and your product. If you fail to have belief in any of these areas, your business is built on shaky ground. As entrepreneurs it's very easy to get sucked up in the naysayers or the negativity. Without belief in yourself and your product you lack the confidence to ever make the sale. You fail to attract the right people to your business because lack of belief in yourself tells others you don't think you can be successful.
- **Flexibility** - When life throws you punches you need to be flexible, especially in business, to handle it. As entrepreneurs we wear many hats. We are a salesperson, accountant, project manager, counselor to team members, trainers and the list goes on. You need to be willing to jump into each aspect of your business from the creative aspects, the tedious tasks and you have to handle the immediate needs. When something in your business isn't working, know when it's time to let it go. If an

opportunity comes up, know when to stop what you're doing and jump on it.

- **Self-Discipline** - When you work from home it's easy to get distracted. You need to know when it's time to work your business and to stick to a schedule. It's also important to have discipline when it comes to your money. Set up a regular pay schedule for yourself so you know when you have money coming into your personal accounts. Don't get caught up in spending money as soon as you make it.
- **Humility** - Confidence is important but you also need to be centered as a leader. It's important you know your business isn't really about you. It's about your customers and your team. When a leader performs from a humble, well-rounded place they are perceived as more honest and trustworthy. An authentic, humble leader leaves their team with a feeling of greatness within themselves.
- **Have a little rebel inside** - You don't need to ride a motorcycle, have tattoos or bright pink hair but you do need to break a few rules when it comes to having a business. Some of the most famous and successful entrepreneurs were told their ideas wouldn't work or they weren't talented or smart enough. But they didn't listen. They forged ahead and did it anyways. Simply by starting a business shows you are going against the majority. Embrace your inner rebel!

These traits, along with your own personality and leadership style, will provide you an easier path to taking the measurable action steps in your journey.

What advice would you give someone who is ready to take their business to the next level?

My best advice for taking your business to the next level is to seek outside help, like a coach or mentor. Investing in your business is the smartest thing an entrepreneur can do but it needs to go beyond purchasing a training program or a free webinar. By hiring an outside coach to work with you one on one, you are able to get an unbiased look at the strengths and weaknesses of your business. A coach also provides a level of accountability that an upline or home office can't provide. A coach who is impartial does not get a direct financial or personal gain from your success. They are there simply because they want to see you succeed and grow.

What is the best description of the relationship between a field member and their corporate office?

I firmly believe each field member is the CEO of their own company and the corporate office is their product supplier. The contract outlines how each member should represent the company but ultimately each field person is responsible for the growth of their own business.

Consistency and reproducible are terms often used by direct sales leaders. What are some of the most successful systems you have seen used by top leaders?

Successful business owners have systems. It's crucial to staying organized, productive and profitable. Some of the most successful systems that I've seen involve a simple 3-ring binder and a calendar. But the most successful system for leaders is learning how to time chunk. Time chunking is blocking out periods of time on your calendar for like tasks. For example, every Monday between 10am – 11am you will run your reports from the previous week. Coaching calls will be done Thursdays between 8am and 12pm. Have a day of the week you complete all of your admin tasks. Put these items on your calendar as if they are an appointment with the doctor or your hairdresser and stick to them. Create a team calendar for coaching calls so your team members can book a call with you easily. This eliminates back and forth texts and calls trying to connect.

It's really easy to get distracted when we are entrepreneurs with busy personal lives or we work from home surrounded by family. Time chunking allows you to have control over your calendar without the chaos or forgetting to complete tasks or even miss calls.

What are some of the big AH-HAs you have seen entrepreneurs experience that then propel them to the next level?

I've worked with direct sales entrepreneurs who struggled with growth and it's often because they have failed to see themselves as anything but a salesperson.

The biggest breakthroughs I see is when they learn to approach their business with a purpose and accept that they have a greater role than a company representative. When an adult toy rep discovers that she has become a confidant for married women who are embarrassed to talk about their relationships she realizes her products were merely a tool she provided and her service was to support the women in their relationship. Her whole outlook on her business changed. She feels like she was her own brand at that very moment. Her purpose was not to sell romance products but it was to teach married women how to communicate more openly and honestly with their partners about sex.

Another example of an entrepreneur "up-leveling" her business was when a skin care representative was talking to me about her business. She revealed that she really felt empowered when she was helping women become more confident in their appearance by having the right skin care regimen. The product itself wasn't what she wanted her business to be about. She wanted to give women the tools and support for building their confidence and self-worth.

My favorite breakthrough that I witnessed was when a cleaning products representative discovered that her true passion was helping women build their dreams of having a successful business. Her purpose with her business was no longer offering healthy cleaning solutions but it was to provide an opportunity for success to women who might not feel supported enough to start their entrepreneurial journey.

By seeing past the product line and realizing that you truly are changing lives with your services, any direct sales entrepreneur has the ability to grow a truly passionate business and has the opportunity to change lives.

What have direct selling entrepreneurs shared with you that they wish they had known when they started?

The number one thing I hear direct sellers share is that they wish someone would've taught them about creating a vision for their business. They started with the hopes of making a few hundred dollars a month. However, once they felt their passion grow and they built their business from a place of purpose; they each felt a shift. The leaders started structuring their business to serve and connect with others, instead of coming from a place to make ends meet for themselves. Each person expressed to me they wish someone had told them their direct sales business was going to be so much more than an income.

What is a characteristic that you have seen that makes you immediately recognize a future leader?

Future leaders quickly recognize their business grows when they approach potential team members from a place of service. Learn how the opportunity serves others. Leaders understand why people join the business and they listen to what their goals and desires are. Even though the business model is designed to be duplicatable, humans are not. It's important to recognize people are motivated and inspired by different things.

What do you see direct sales leaders do to keep motivated and encouraging of their team when things aren't going right?

Leading by example and being transparent yet maintaining a level of professionalism with your team is the perfect way to keep a team motivated; even when it seems like business is tough. I've seen one of two things happen with leaders - they either continue to pretend everything in the business is going great (trying not to scare their team members) or they treat everything as if it's all going to fail.

Leaders need to show when they are having challenges but they don't need to react as if the sky is falling. If someone on your team is having a great month but you start telling everyone how bad the economy is, the positive team members will start to feel guilty or worried. While the people who haven't been doing well look at the economy as an excuse to not work as hard. You don't always have to be on stuffy, or boring behavior but you must be leading by example.

What are the mistakes you have seen leaders make that stifle the growth of their teams?

Leaders, especially new leaders, are so determined to support their team members that they often do things for them, instead of showing them how to do it for themselves. They want to appear as though they are there for their team but they are actually hurting them. In order for a team member to become a leader they need to know how to teach their team.

Most new leaders don't realize new team members want to emulate them. This is especially true when their leader is successful. If something is working for their leader, they want to do it for their own business. If a team member sees their leader hovering or being too controlling, they learn to believe that's how they must act in order to grow, which is quite the opposite.

What are the biggest surprises/hurdles entrepreneurs face once they become leaders?

The biggest hurdles I feel new leaders have is with time management and boundaries with their team. I see many leaders get caught in the trap of not having office hours and taking team member calls at any time. The problem with this habit is it's extremely easy to feel like you need to always be there for your team. In reality, a great leader helps to empower. By setting clear office hours, you are teaching your team to respect your time, you are respecting your own time, as well as your family's time. You also teach team members to search for answers themselves instead of always relying on you. Office hours allow for entrepreneurs to plan their schedule.

In talking about boundaries, a very common challenge is when a new leader cannot differentiate a team member from a friend. While I strongly encourage connection with your team and building camaraderie and trust, I feel it's equally important to maintain a level of professionalism so you can keep friendship and business completely separate. I've seen many business relationships ruin teams because a friendship has gone awry.

How do successful entrepreneurs create a direct sales business that perpetuates?

As with a business in any industry the most successful entrepreneurs build their business from a place of service and authenticity. Be authentic in how you connect with others. Come from a place of helping those who might need it, instead of pitching your products. For example, if you're at a networking event and you overhear someone talking about her dry skin, you probably might say "Oh my gosh, I sell a super-awesome product for $29.95. Do you want to buy some?". Instead of coming at the person with your products, bring your service into the conversation by offering help. You might rather say "Did you know dry skin is usually caused by dehydration or change in weather. If you find that drinking more water still doesn't help, I would love to chat with you about some additional options that I could offer." This approach is going to sound and feel much less slimy. People will want to connect with and refer you more often, which will increase your longevity and your profits.

What is the one key piece of advice you have given to the leaders you coach that has proven the most successful?

Be the CEO of your own business has been the greatest successful piece of advice I have given to leaders - advice I originally heard from our own Teresa Garrison. Step into the power of being an entrepreneur instead of playing small, under the thumb of your corporate office. Once you can harness your own power and purpose, the possibilities of growing your business truly are infinite. I've seen direct sales leaders morph into business and life coaches. I've witnessed leaders create their own voice and their own brand by stepping into this powerful mindset. When this happens they are creating an authentic brand and stand out in a very busy sea of sales reps.

What is the best investment you have seen direct sales entrepreneurs make in themselves?

Hiring a coach is the best investment I've seen direct sales entrepreneurs make. When you start a business it's a personal development journey as much as it is a professional one. With the internet it's really easy to hit Google to look for advice or tips for growing your business. The problem with this strategy is Google doesn't know your business. Hiring a coach becomes a personal investment. A coach is interested in the details of your business and your vision.

If you were standing in front of 200 new field members who just joined a direct sales company what 3 things would you share?

If I were to stand in a room of 200 brand new field members, I would tell them the following three things:

Right now, right this very minute decide that your business is more than just a hobby. You are now holding the opportunity and the power to create a legacy for yourself, your family and for other people. Do not limit yourself and don't be afraid to dream big. If you have dreams to hang out on a yacht and drink champagne, then go after that. The direct sales industry is a gateway for you to build your own empire. You are being handed the tools and support that most entrepreneurs don't receive until they hire a coach. You don't have to stop at an extra $500 a month. You don't have to be the "additional income" for your household. You have the power within you, right now, to decide your business will be so much more than that.

Set goals. Create a vision for yourself. Don't just go through the motions with your business and then wonder why it's not working. Create a plan and then work that plan like your children's lives depend on it. Your business is not an optional activity. So put on that role of business owner, of CEO and rock it!

Ask for help! Don't feel like you are in this alone. Ask your upline to help you. Contact your corporate office. Hire a coach. Read a business book if you need to. You are in an industry that is all about lifting each other up. If you can't talk to your upline or your sponsor, find someone you can talk to.

Maybe the help you need isn't with your business. Maybe you're overwhelmed with the housework. Ask your partner or spouse to do an extra chore. Hire a cleaning service or exchange services for products. Sometimes the greatest help we can get for our business is someone to help us around the house or to babysit the kids.

Too many times I see entrepreneurs, especially women, feel they need to handle everything like a super woman. It's okay to raise your hand and say "Hey! I need a little help over here."

What have you learned about yourself while working with top leaders in the direct sales industry?

Working with leaders in the direct sales industry has taught me that I am very passionate about women in business succeeding. This is the fuel that puts the fire in my belly and the entire mission my business is founded on. A passion that I don't think I would've realized had I not been surrounded by such motivated and driven women who encourage others to be successful. I think it's a beautiful thing when women shift into the mindset of believing in herself as an entrepreneur.

How does your expertise help someone building a direct sales business?

With over 20 years of small business experience, including 6 years with the corporate office of a million dollar direct sales business; I have been able to help direct sales professionals create strategies that allow them to automate more of their business so they can connect with a greater portion of their customers and teams. I have a strong public relations background and I coach my clients on how to pitch and present themselves to the media. With my marketing experience I have the specialty of working with a professional to get really clear on what her personal brand message is so she can stand out in a very busy sea of other direct sellers.

What are the top 3 things you would recommend, based on your expertise, that accelerates business growth?

The top 3 things I would recommend for accelerating business growth are:

- Create your own personal brand - stand out from all of the other company representatives by having a unique message. Don't call yourself an independent rep. Create a title for what you are about in your business. Decide what you want to be known for.
- Pick a Niche - Dig deep into who you really love having as a part of your business - as both customer and team member. Make the decision to become an authority with a small group instead of trying to be a little fish in a big pond and get lost. Too many direct sellers try to sell to everyone and end up selling to nobody because their message is too generic. By creating a niche, you can tailor your marketing and sales messages to meet the specific needs of your customers.
- Believe in yourself as an entrepreneur - Contrary to what you may have heard, direct sellers are so much more than a product rep. You have control over your calendar, your income, and your team. The corporate office only provides you with tools to use and the product you sell. However, they do not define your success. You define your success by believing in your products, your services and yourself. When you have faith in who you are as a business owner you will attract more people who want to do business with you.

Continue the Conversation with Desiree Wolfe:

 Known as The Rebel Mamapreneur, Desiree Wolfe teaches women in the Direct Sales Industry to break rules and think like a CEO. With over 20 years of business experience she has taken her knowledge to the coaching world. She believes that every woman can succeed in business and have a family if she's given the right tools and support. You can find her teaching time-saving and online growth strategies at www.DesireeWolfe.com

Below are the various ways that you can connect with Desiree and learn more about what she has to offer.

- **Website:**
  www.DesireeWolfe.com

- **Twitter:**
  www.twitter.com/DesireeMktg

- **Facebook:**
  www.facebook.com/TheDesireeWolfe

LYNDSEY BAIGENT
Founder, Party Plan Revolution

Share with us what your business is and why you focus on supporting the direct sales industry?

When I first started in direct sales I had two children one of whom has cerebral palsy and autism. My husband worked away from home for extended periods of time. Although I had his financial support I often felt as though I was a single parent. Autism is unpredictable and I needed a flexible career that enabled me to take care of the challenges associated with autism as they arose.

Raising a child with special needs wasn't something my husband or I had planned. Few parents ever do. I struggled emotionally and turned to food, alcohol and gambling as a way to escape from the emotional turmoil I felt.

In December 2003 I hit rock bottom. I was fat, broke and desperately unhappy. I remember my darkest moment sitting on the back patio of our home in Brisbane with a packet of sleeping tablets in one hand, a wine in the other seriously contemplating taking my own life. Then as fate would have it I heard my daughter's school bus come down the street. Wiping the tears from my eyes I went to meet her. She greeted me differently that day. Reaching for my hand she looked me in the eye and said "you'll never leave me mum will you?"

In that moment I decided I would do whatever it took to turn my life around. I didn't know how I was going to do it but I knew I'd find a way. I stopped drinking and smoking immediately. Although I made the decision to quit gambling the same day, it took 18 months for me to completely kick the habit.

As I began my recovery journey I started to notice that many other people were struggling emotionally. I could see the pain in the eyes of women at my parties. When working with my team I quickly realized that their struggle to succeed had little to do with lack of business skills. Lack of self-awareness, confidence, self-belief and the ability to navigate the emotional roller coaster of life was the issue. I knew that unless I was able to help people grow in these areas no amount of training on how to get bookings, sell or recruit would produce the success they desired and deserved. I made a promise to myself that when I got my own life back on track I would pay forward what I was learning to help others. Growing in self-awareness is a daily practice for me and has become the foundation of my work with Direct Sellers. The results…more bookings, higher sales, stronger team growth and a happier more fulfilled life.

What is your favorite thing about the direct sales industry?

I love that direct sales provides a supportive playground for personal growth and financial freedom. If you're willing to get in the game and play full out, everything is possible.

What is the most rewarding aspect of working with direct sales entrepreneurs?

Direct sellers have the potential to make a huge difference in the world not just as a result of what they sell but as a result of who they become. My favorite quote of all time is 'be the change you want to see in the world'. It's one of the key foundations of how I choose to live my own life and something I pay forward through my Party Plan Academy. When direct sellers choose to embrace this concept the ripple effect is massive. This is what excites me the most!

What do you consider great characteristics of successful entrepreneurs?

1. They know that stretching themselves is part of the journey toward greater success and are comfortable with feeling uncomfortable.
2. They live life with an attitude of gratitude.
3. They are solutions orientated and choose to focus on problems just long enough to understand them so they can quickly find a way forward.
4. They have defined healthy personal boundaries and are not afraid to uphold them.
5. They are active listeners who ask questions in order to better understand how they can be of service to others.

What are your insights about the direct selling industry that will best help people build a strong business?

Irrespective of what company direct sellers are aligned with the direct sales business model is relatively simple. There are only so many ways you can book, sell and recruit. What makes our industry complex is the people component. People are the heart of any direct sales business. The more invested direct sellers become in understanding themselves and the people they have the privilege of serving through their business the more successful they will become.

What advice would you give someone who is ready to take their business to the next level?

Make personal growth a way of life. Read books, attend seminars, get a mentor or a coach and surround yourself with people who will inspire you to become more as an individual. Your business will only grow if you do.

Consistency and reproducible are terms often used by direct sales leaders. What are some of the most successful systems you have seen used by top leaders?

I stumbled over a great acronym the other that describes the role of systems beautifully. You may have seen it before but just in case you haven't I thought I'd share it with you.

SYSTEMS - Save You Substantial Time Energy and Money.

Here's what I believe to be the three most important things to consider when choosing effective systems for your direct sales business.

1. Simplicity

In 2012 I created a Natural Gift Assessment as a tool to help direct sellers understand their unique strengths so as to make the journey toward success easier and more fun. With more than 10,000 direct sellers having taken the assessment it's provided me with some great insights about what direct sellers need to learn and the best way to teach it.

One of my most surprising discoveries was that less than 5% of direct sellers have what I call 'The Gift Of Technology'. This means that any system that involves technology had to be extremely simple.

2. Automation

The whole idea of having systems is to, save you substantial time energy and money. Right? This means that any system you choose needs to have a component of automation. Whether it's being able to create your email newsletter and schedule it to be sent on a specific day and time or having a specific email sequence triggered the moment you enter someone's name into your data base or creating a list of host coaching tasks the moment you enter an upcoming party. This type of automation makes running your business easy and more time efficient.

3. Duplication

It's been my observation that there are a lot more direct sellers willing to follow systems than are able or perhaps willing to create them. What does this mean in terms of duplication?

It means that if you want to support your team to achieve greater levels of success you must be willing to be the one to create systems. To maximize the ripple effect of duplication, systems need to be simple for your team to implement and easy for you to share.

Let's take host coaching as an example.

If you have a step by step process that results in more parties holding, you can teach your team the steps but unless you can provide a system that reminds them to implement the steps then it's likely that only a very small percentage of your team will take consistent action. While many of your team may have good intentions to implement what they've learned it's been my observation that few will follow through.

If you can provide your team with a simple way to implement your step by step host coaching system, then they are more likely to follow through and do what you know works!

So does such a system exist? The answer is YES! When I started looking for systems that offered simplicity, automation and duplication I couldn't find anything that ticked all three boxes. So I decided to create one. It's called My Party Plan Biz.

I encourage you to check it out at www.MyPartyPlanBiz.com.

What are some of the big AH-HAs you have seen direct sales entrepreneurs experience that then propel them to the next level?

I've had the privilege of witnessing many AHA moments over the years. Here's one that I know has been very impactful for many direct sellers. It's around 'fear of the phone'. I'm not sure if you've noticed but it seems that there is an epidemic of direct sellers out there who have some sort of fear when it comes to the phone. Yet whenever I see direct sellers at their training, conventions or at my events, their phone is never far away. Kind of curious don't you think?

So I did a little research on the topic and it seems that very few people have a true fear of the phone. This is known as phone phobia; those who do are afraid of making and receiving calls from anyone. Having worked with direct sellers for more than 15 years I can't recall having met anyone who fits this description.

So when I'm working with direct sellers and they tell me they have a 'fear of the phone' I ask them this question. If I gave you a list of ten people's names and phone numbers and told you that when you make all ten calls the following will happen:

- 2 people will ask for a catalogue
- 3 people won't be home so you'll get their voicemail
- 1 person will hang up on you
- 1 person will book a party
- 2 people will be pleased you called but won't take any further action
- 1 person will ask for information about joining your team would you make the phone calls?

Whenever I ask this question, direct sellers sound surprised, sometimes almost shocked as they say … of course! My response is … didn't you just tell me you were scared to make calls? What I've come to learn is that it's not making the phone calls that most people are afraid of even though they will say it is. What they are fearful of is the 'UNCERTAINTY' of making the phone calls. The moment you remove the uncertainty and assure people of the outcome they are willing to make the calls.

One thing I know for sure is …

If you want to create a successful direct sales business, you must be willing to become comfortable with uncertainty.

What is a characteristic that you have seen that makes you immediately recognize a future leader?

Two that spring to mind immediately are self-awareness and a desire to be of service to others.

What do you see direct sales leaders do to keep motivated and encouraging of their team when things aren't going right?

I have a favorite question I share with leaders that has really helped keep my motivation alive when things aren't going right. They've told me that it's really helped them during challenging times, so I'd like to share that with you today. The question is: What's great about this?

No matter how bad things may seem if you choose to look for what's great you'll find it. Asking this question quickly shifts your thinking from one of doom and gloom to one of hope and possibility. Try it yourself, then share it with your team, I'm sure you'll find it very helpful in quickly moving to a more positive place.

I've also found it really useful to remember that motivation is an emotional state that we move in and out of just like any other emotional state. There are times when we feel our motivational spark burning brightly and times when we question whether it exists at all. So what do you need to do when you feel like you've lost your motivation?

Here's my simple three step process:

Step 1. Reboot Your Energy

When you lack motivation your energy can be quite heavy. Sometimes it can feel like a cloudy day, other times it's like a full blown thunder storm. The first step is to shift your energy. The quickest and easiest way to do this is by moving your body. This can be as simple as going for a walk around the house or in the garden, or dancing to your favorite music, going for a run, or jumping on the kid's trampoline. It doesn't matter what movement you choose but you must MOVE!

Step 2. Rekindle Magic Moments

With your eyes closed and a gentle smile on your face start to remember the moments in your business where you have felt most proud, excited, happy, joyful and grateful. Think of a really funny time where you laughed so hard that you risked stuff flying out of your nose. Think of a time where you knew in your heart you had made a real difference in someone else's life. Remember a time where you felt a deep sense of connection with your team.   Recall a sacred time where you felt your life was guided by a power much greater than you.

Play these magic moments in your mind's eye like a movie. Make the images big and bright, hear the sounds you heard and smell the smells you smelled. Flood your body with the positive feelings of these magic moments. Gently open your eyes and take a moment to savour the memories and the great feelings flowing through your body.

Step 3. Refocus Your Thinking

Feeling great, ask yourself these three questions:

1. Why am I committed to creating a successful business?
2. Who will I become in the process? more confident, organized etc.
3. Other than me, who else will benefit as a result of my success?

I've taken many people who have lost their motivation through this process and it works great. So next time you lose your motivation, give it a try.

What are the mistakes you've seen leaders make that stifle the growth of their teams?

I'd say the top three mistakes I've seen leaders make are ...

1. They fail to ask enough questions often making assumptions based on their own experience about what things mean.

For example:

A new team member says I want to work my business full time. Instead of asking what 'full time' means for that team member the leader makes an assumption based on what 'full time' means for them.

2. They focus too much on what they want instead of on the goals, dreams and desires of their team. Remember the saying by Zig Ziglar – 'you will get all you want in life, if you help enough other people get what they want".

3. They become too emotionally involved with members of their team which adversely impacts their ability to be an effective coach and mentor.

What are the biggest surprises/hurdles entrepreneurs face once they become leaders?

I think one of the biggest hurdles direct sales entrepreneurs have to face is finding the balance between working their personal business and supporting their team. So often when direct sellers first start growing their team they take their eye off their personal business and focus all their time and energy on helping their team. If you have a career plan that involves your team breaking away from you when they reach a particular level, you must continue to grow your personal business. Failing to do so can end up costing you financially and emotionally. I remember when I was in the field I fell into this trap. It cost me my company car!

Here's a couple of tips to prevent you from falling into this trap:-

1. Schedule time each week to work on growing your personal business.

2. Be smart with your time. Wherever possible invite members of your team to 'shadow' you while you're working your personal business. Share a list of party dates with your team so they see you working your personal business and so they know when and where your parties are so they can select a date to come along. Invite upcoming leaders to be on the phone with you when you're coaching and mentoring members of your team. This will ensure maximum time efficiency for you and optimum learning for your team.

3. Outsource activities that you don't enjoy doing and that can be done by others. The more your business grows the more help you'll need. Don't be afraid to pay someone to help you. The more time you invest on income producing activities the more money you'll have to pay people to help you.

How do successful entrepreneurs create a direct sales business that perpetuates?

If you want to create a direct sales business that perpetuates spend 80% of your time being of service to the people you have already done business with and 20% of your time finding new people to do business with. Having systems that support this process makes it achievable no matter how big your business becomes.

When you take care of people, you'll be surprised at how willing they are to refer new people to you. The result – endless bookings, increased sales and rapid team growth.

What is the one key piece of advice you have given to the leaders you coach that has proven the most successful?

Help your team members get what they want from their business and as a result you'll get what you want. You can't be successful in this industry without helping others experience success. It's one of the things I really love about our industry.

What is the best investment you have seen direct sales entrepreneurs make in themselves?

I think one of the best investments direct sales entrepreneurs can make is to hire the services of a coach. Working from home can be tough even with great support from your company. When you have a coach as part of your team they will shine a light on things you can't see about yourself so you continue to grow and evolve.

To be honest, most of the coaching I do with top leaders has nothing to do with business. If they are already leaders, they usually know what to do to create a successful business.

Let me ask you this ...

If you're in an intimate relationship that isn't working will that impact your ability to be your best in business?

If your relationship with money is all about scarcity and survival will that impact your ability to take your business to new heights?

If you don't treat your body with respect and as a result are constantly lacking energy, will that impact your ability to grow your business?

If you run scared every time conflict arises will that affect your ability to effectively lead your team?

If you struggle to say 'no' and choose to spend most of your time helping other people, will that impact your ability to turn your own dreams into reality?

I think you'll agree the answer is ... YES!

You are the foundation of your business. If you're not willing to strengthen and grow your foundations, you're unlikely to take your business to great heights.

If you were standing in front of 200 new field members who just joined a direct sales company what 3 things would you share?

If you want to achieve success in your business, there are three key areas you need to master.

1. Your Mindset

Having worked with thousands of direct sales entrepreneurs over the years, it's become obvious that those who succeed have a pattern of thinking that supports their success. Those who struggle have a pattern of thinking that supports their struggle. Becoming aware of your patterns of thought including the stories you tell yourself is the first step in creating a mindset that will support your success.

2. Your Energy

It's my belief that thoughts create emotion, emotion creates energy and energy fuels action. Energy + Action = Results

If you take the right action with the wrong energy you're not going to get the best results. So what do I mean by energy? All emotions have energy. Emotions such as disappointment, anger, and frustration have a heavy dark energy. Emotions such as gratitude, enthusiasm and hope have a light bright energy. It is this energy not your words that greets people when you first meet them. You can take all the right action but if you fuel it with the wrong energy you will struggle to get the results you want in your business.

3. Time

One of the most challenging aspects of working from home is being effective with your time. Here's my top three tips for improving your time management:

1. When you start working from home it's likely that people around you may have the perception you have lots of time on your hands and are therefore available to do things with them or for them at a moment's notice. Setting boundaries and learning to say no can be difficult, especially with those close to you, however it's a must if you want to work successfully from home.

2. Create a plan for how you choose to spend your time. There are 168 hours in every week. How you choose to spend them is up to you. Be sure to choose wisely!

3. When working from home it's easy to get distracted by things around you. Identify your distractions and do whatever it takes to minimize the impact they have on your ability to work your business effectively.

What have you learned about yourself while working with top leaders in the direct sales industry?

Working with leaders in the direct sales industry inspires me to dig deep and keep striving to become the best version of myself possible. I am reminded every day of the privilege it is to serve and feel incredibly blessed and grateful that I have found my calling in life.

How does your expertise help someone building a direct sales business?

Human behavior is my specialty. I believe the more we understand about what makes people do what they do the more we are to help them be successful and as a result become successful ourselves.

I am constantly in search of new ways to support direct sales entrepreneurs get a better understanding of what makes them tick so they can make a bigger difference in the world. Let's face it, there are only so many ways to book, sell and recruit. People are the heart of any direct sales business. If we want to become more successful we need to become committed to getting a better understanding of people.

To date I've spent close to $100,000 learning from some of the best teachers in the world. Personal growth is a way of life for me. I walk my talk and as a result what I teach works in the real world.

What are the top 3 things you would recommend, based on your expertise, that accelerates business growth?

I know I've said it many times before but I'm going to say it again …

1. Make personal growth a way of life. The more you grow the more your business will grow.

2. Spend 80% of your time learning about people and 20% of your time learning about business. The heart of every direct sales business is people. So make learning all you can about people your focus.

3. Focus on serving others. The more you support others to get what they want the more you will get what you want.

Continue the Conversation with Lyndsey Baigent:

Lyndsey Baigent is an international speaker, coach and trainer. Her mission, is to help Party Planners end their struggle for bookings and create a profitable business they love. Known as The Booking Queen, Lyndsey went from having no bookings in her calendar to being booked out three to four months in advance doing an average of 20-25 parties a month. In her craziest month she did 42 parties. If Lyndsey can do it ... you can too!

Below are the various ways that you can connect with Lyndsey and learn more about what she has to offer.

- **Website:**
  www.partyplanrevolution.com

- **Facebook:**
  www.facebook.com/PartyPlanRevolution

DEB BIXLER
Founder, CashFlowShow.com

Tell us a little about yourself and how you were first introduced to the direct sales industry?

I worked in the food service industry for 30 years and had come to a point in my life where I was getting sick and tired of being sick and tired. The stress was killing me!

I was looking for something new when I got invited to my very first home party. The consultant said: "Watch what I do here today and for those of you who would like to make money and have fun with MyFantasticCompany, just get with me after the show and I will be glad to give you more information!" The seed was planted.

A couple of months later I took a reduced responsibility (50% pay cut) position that only required a 40 hour work week at my job and joined the company. I worked both my full-time job and my party plan business for nine months with a mission to date one home party every day. (And I did!) After retiring from the corporate world entirely I went on to use my party plan business as my total household income for seven years.

Share with us what your business is and why you focus on supporting the direct sales industry?

Basically, at the Cash Flow Show, we teach best business practices that all successful companies use as they are applied to the party plan business model. The Cash Flow Show is a series of systems that work in all direct sales businesses. When applied to your business you will create a consistent cash flow from your home business.

When you treat your business with the same respect that you would treat your JOB (Jump Out of Bed JOB) you will get the same results! This is a simple business model and it will work for anyone who works it using proven systems. Businesses never fail, people never fail... only systems fail. If you are not getting the results, you want then get a new system!!

What is your favorite thing about the direct sales industry?

I get to sleep as late as I want and I don't even have an alarm clock in my bedroom any more....

Seriously though:

I have always loved to teach so as a leader the aspect of team-building, teaching at parties and changing peoples' lives was just as exciting as my previous career. I now teach others how to treat their business like a professional and use the same best business practices and party plan systems that gave me success in the industry. Anyone can "Create A Cash Flow Show" party plan business! Get it? Create a cash flow party plan show schedule using systems!

What is the most rewarding aspect of working with direct sales entrepreneurs?

I love hearing that a direct seller took the Cash Flow Show systems and applied them to their business and they worked!! They WILL WORK for everyone who works them! Truly a replicable system of party plan presentation!!! LOVE it!

What is your definition of a successful direct sales entrepreneur?

A successful entrepreneur is neither needy nor desperate for business.

What do you consider great characteristics of successful entrepreneurs?

A work at home entrepreneur must be self-motivated, committed and willing to treat their business like a professional. Professionalism is an attitude, not a time commitment. Whether you want to work your party plan business part-time, full-time or even less, you WILL create a consistent cash flow show working from home when you have a professional attitude.

What advice would you give someone who is ready to take their business to the next level?

A personal coach who has been there/done that is essential. Whether it be your upline, cross line, or a private outside resource, having a coach who matches your style and goals is vital and will leverage your results. The important thing is that you pick one carefully by doing your research.

Does the potential coach speak, write and teach on YOUR topics? Does the coach have both business experience AND coaching/mentoring experience? A mentor can have all the credentials in the world and if their style does not match your personality, then it won't work. With good research to find the right business growth coach your money will be returned in multiples.

What is the best description of the relationship between a field member and their corporate office?

A great company provides great support and recognizes that their field is the most important customer. The field distributor values and respects the brand and emulates company policy to leverage the support provided by the company.

(more below)

Consistency and reproducible are terms often used by direct sales leaders. What are some of the most successful systems you have seen used by top leaders?

Well of course the Cash Flow Show party plan training system!! Aside from that: Your company has put time, money and energy into creating support for you. Don't recreate the wheel; use what they have created on all levels. Getting your team member off to a great start is key! Getting your new consultant off to a great start can sometimes be as simple as using the super starter kit the way it was designed!

The company had a well-thought-out plan when they put together the kit so use it as a tool to set the bar for new consultant expectations. Refer to the kit in your new consultant training just like you would refer a hostess to the hostess benefit package.
The more you can get your new consultant into the kit the more quickly they will take action!

Another example of leveraging the kit is to use the hostess benefit flier in training. The hostess benefit flier usually has a chart or worksheet for the hostess to use to list as many people as possible to invite to the party. Suggest that the consultant get out the hostess flier and use it to explain the benefits to them. Then ask the new consultant to create a list using the same hostess memory jogging sheet to help them think of who they should plan to contact about their new business.

Get your new distributor into the kit by reinforcing what the company has focused on. Use words that set the same expectations that the company did. On the first call to your new distributor or even when interviewing the potential consultant before they join, you may say things like:

Reference the literature that reinforces the bars that the corporate office has set. The bonus fliers, the hostess benefit package, the compensation plan literature are all in the kit for a reason. Most likely there is a 'fast start' checklist of some sort.... clear instructions of what to do first! Use it to your advantage by communicating with your new team member with the same messages!

What are some of the big AH-HAs you have seen entrepreneurs experience that then propel them to the next level?

Starting a new business is like getting a train moving...

It takes an effort but you can't stop a moving train!! After it is rolling along it is effortless and that is the same in home businesses.

When a distributor sees a system working and they come to realize that all that work is paying off...

Yippee! The systems are working!!!

What have direct selling entrepreneurs shared with you that they wish they had known when they started?

That they cannot depend on friends and family!! No business should really! Your company probably gave you the directive to write down your top 100 or so people that you have ever known since kindergarten and call them! Right!? LOL.

That is a good place to start but no business can survive on just family and friends. We must first put down a solid root system for our business using every category pictured on this business tree.
When first starting your business, focus on securing shows or customers in all the different categories so that your home business is solidly rooted.

There are many ways to generate business including:

- Friends
- Family
- Schools
- Work
- Neighbors
- Organizations
- Churches/Synagogues
- Home Party
- Strangers

Use the business tree concept and combine it with the sales funnel (many lead generation systems and building relationships) and you will never worry about finding business again! The taproot for your tree is generating leads with strangers. This turns into your business tree trunk above ground. All the other people/leads/streams of income, including those you meet at your home parties, are "acquaintances."

Balanced Business Using the Business Tree

A balanced business generates income from all of the above sources of business and then has a root and a branch for each one. A solid business tree will stand the test of time. If your business tree does not have a root for each source of leads, then your tree will eventually fall over. When a direct sales business consultant runs a balanced business, they have lead generation techniques that bring in a continuous stream of leads from a wide variety of sources.

If you ONLY depend on family and friends for business, you will only have two roots on your tree and then only two income branches/streams. Sooner or later the tree will fall over! Your business will fail! Even if you have been in business for a while, you can always start over. Starting your home party business with a specific focus on each group will ensure that your business tree never falls over! Put down a strong business taproot by seeking strangers for customers. Teach your sales team how to find strangers for their home business. Train your new consultants to have their first 20 shows fall into each category.

What is a characteristic that you have seen that makes you immediately recognize a future leader?

Good leaders consistently invest time and/or money to improve their leadership skills. To be an inspiration to your team members there are certain things a sales leader must do. The good news is these skills can be acquired through ongoing work and education.

Good leaders must be willing to grow through the never-ending process of study, education, and training. Leaders encourage their teams to create success by being credible and by challenging team members. They always search for opportunities to experiment and take risks that inspire others by envisioning the future and helping others to visualize their own vision for their future.

- A leader has personal integrity; people know that she or he can be counted on to follow through on commitments, avoid conflicts of interest and adhere to the rules, regulations and ethical codes of the profession.
- A leader is a good communicator and understands the people they're trying to reach.
- A leader is a masterful listener.
- A leader has tenacity, strength of will and never gives up.
- A leader inspires others to be the best they can be.
- A leader demonstrates commitment to ongoing support and mentoring.
- A leader motivates by helping people understand the value of working towards shared or personal goals.
- A leader models enthusiasm, teamwork and authenticity.
- A leader respects others and themselves.
- A leader learns by continuing education and training and professional development.
- A leader stays current in the industry and is open to learning from others.
- A leader builds strong teams with confidence.
- A leader enables a team to foster collaboration and strengthen others by modeling that behavior themselves.

- A leader plans for small, ongoing successes while encouraging and celebrating accomplishments along the way.
- A leader maintains a positive mental attitude no matter what the circumstances and acts with initiative and courage.
- A leader strives to be the best at all times, to speak in a positive and professional manner and demonstrates commitment in words, actions and appearance.
- A leader treats people respectfully, understands and accommodates differences, and respects confidentiality.
- A leader, by positive example, endlessly fosters a team environment in which all team members can reach their highest potential.
- A leader encourages the team to reach team goals as effectively as possible, while also working tirelessly to strengthen the bonds among the various members.

What do you see direct sales leaders do to keep motivated and encouraging of their team when things aren't going right?

If I could put motivation into a gift bag, I would gladly "gift" it to everyone I know in direct sales! However, reality is very different. You can inspire others, but motivation isn't something you can give to another. Motivation comes from within oneself.

"When you know what you want and want it bad enough, you will find a way to get it."
Jim Rohn

How to Motivate a Team

It is easier to tell you how you CANNOT motivate your consultants than it is to say how you can motivate! While everyone needs money it is not a motivator! However, lack of it will cause de-motivation. Underutilization of skills is a de-motivator as well. When a person applies their skills to the fullest they tend to be more motivated. Too much stress reduces motivation and lack of any stress at all leads to laziness. It is difficult to create a definitive post on how to motivate a team because each individual on the team is unique. This is a topic that greater minds than Deb Bixler have analyzed for centuries!

An Engaged Team Is a Motivated Team

The key to motivation is to find out what drives each member of your sales team, then keep them engaged. Keeping your team engaged is key to motivation! Perform your team meeting planning (both online and off) with the idea of team growth in the forefront of your mind and engage every personality.

Each team member has to be a part of the bigger picture as well as their own home business goals. Do you have a bigger team goal? How is each member a part of the bigger picture? Consider each team member a leader from the beginning and treat them as such! "Every soldier is a leader regardless of his rank or position." Department of the Army pamphlet 600-64. Platoon sergeants are expected to be ready and able to take command of a platoon in the platoon leader's absence. Non-commissioned officers are expected to show initiative – to get things done without waiting to be told by a superior. Manage your team with an eye toward each person's own advancement into management.

The Basics of How to Motivate Your Team!

Be a leader and emulate a leadership attitude! The classic statement of lead by example is true in direct sales too! Don't expect your team members to be high performers if you are not! Coach in private – Praise in public! Confidence is always bolstered with public recognition. Remember to recognize the person, not the deed! DEED Recognition: "Wow! Look at Lisa – congratulations on a $1000 show!"

PERSONAL Recognition: "Wow! Let's give Lisa a round of applause for taking the extra time to connect with her hostesses! Can you give us one tip on what you did to have a $1000 show?!" Incorporate recognition awards into your routine that support those that are not high achievers as well! When you proactively encourage all members of your team it will generate enthusiasm that will inspire everyone to work or achieve more.

Run incentives – especially ones that get them to the corporate events! If your company already runs incentives, make sure that you incentivize their incentives. Piggy-back what you do off the home office incentives. Too many incentives can do just the opposite of what you want, so leverage the corporate efforts! Create incentives that encourage meeting attendance for your local and regional meetings and also the company-wide conferences. Conference incentives that are run annually on the team level should hype up conference interest!

If I were to say one single thing that is the secret formula on how to motivate your team, I would say – Get them to national conference! Take genuine interest in your team! Go for friendship! When you become friends and create an environment that encourages friendships, your team will keep coming back for more. A good listener is always perceived as being genuine! Take the time to listen. You do not have to always be nagging them about moving up the ladder or doing more. When you know what each team member wants and guide each with measurable actions toward their goals, they will stay engaged.

Delegate, Delegate, Delegate! The direct sales leader who does it all is the direct sales team leader that does it all by themselves! Your team has many personalities and skills. By delegating tasks and utilizing your team as the leaders that they are becoming it makes your job easier and may motivate them from within.

Teach Basic Booking Skills First

No one quits when they are making money. Put a strong system of teaching your distributors to become expert schedulers and everything else will follow. Every consultant should be trained on how to grow a strong business tree at the very first training session! The single most important thing for a new consultant to learn is how to find business! Never complain down! There is nothing that can de-motivate a team more than a negative word from their upline (you). If you have a problem, complaint or issue always pass your concerns up the ladder not down!

Motivating Your Sales Team

Inspiring your team IS the job description for leading a team. If you figure out how to motivate a team you will be able to sell your secret and become rich!! LOL Each person on your sales team is motivated differently. Motivation comes from within and from a belief in one's dream. Find out what that dream is, keep them engaged, show them the path to make that dream a reality, and they become motivated!

What are the mistakes you have seen leaders make that stifle the growth of their teams?

A great leader who has a great team is one who has a balanced business and uses all resources for income and lead generation. (see above)

- Mistakes?
- Complain!! You can complain up but never down!!
- Expect to share the opportunity ONLY and not do home parties!
- Only work online!

What are the biggest surprises/hurdles entrepreneurs face once they become leaders?

Many distributors hold back on leadership because they feel that it may be too much work... they are too busy already but in fact it is not going to take any more time than already invested to make the same amount of money when you utilize a systematic – replicable approach to creating a caring and sharing team.

I recommend that everyone take on the duties of a leader BEFORE they are a leader. This gives the potential new leader the ability to practice and or create the systems emulated by the upline and/or created by the company on a smaller scale.

How do successful entrepreneurs create a direct sales business that perpetuates?

Business momentum is what it takes to create a self-perpetuating business! Think about a train... it is hard to get it moving but when it is rolling along, momentum makes it easy to keep on going! It is tough to stop a moving train! Your business is the same! It takes effort to get it going but once you have it rolling along, life gets easier!

Create Business Momentum! When does this get easier?!! When you have your ideal show schedule in place and keep it that way by actually performing that many shows for three consecutive months you will develop a self-perpetuating business! Business momentum will kick in because you will be standing in front of the majority of your future hosts at your parties.

What is your ideal show schedule? Put it in place allowing for 25% cancellations and perform your ideal show schedule three months in a row. At that point, your outside activities will be less than your show activities because you will be meeting most of your new shows at existing shows. Then the networking activities which you perform outside your party will keep new blood coming in to keep your business tree strong.

The Cash Flow Show party plan training program is founded in systems that create business momentum so that your business train never stops rolling! Many direct sellers quit before their business begins to self-perpetuate because they expected it to be easy! Everything good involves effort! Put the time and effort into it, don't quit and it will pay off!

What is the one key piece of advice you have given to the leaders you coach that has proven the most successful?

Whether you want full time, part time or just a bit of extra money, it is a system of leadership attitudes and business practices that will lead to success. You can be a leader or a needer… It's a personal choice. Do you need people to do business with you or do you run a successful, service-focused business? Are you leaning more toward the needy side or the leader's side? Success is an attitude. If you are constantly struggling with your business, maybe you deserve to reconsider your focus and create an attitude adjustment for yourself. Move your thoughts and actions to the success based side of life and change your "luck".

Your attitude is a choice!

You can change your attitude anytime you want!

YOU are in control of your "ATTITUDE."

YOU are in control of your achievements.

YOU are in control of your earnings.

YOU are in control of your business.

YOU are in control of your success.

If you were standing in front of 200 new field members who just joined a direct sales company what 3 things would you share?

Like a real job... there are not secrets to success! Just get up every day and go to work. Put systems in place to make things run smoothly. Use every lead generation system available to you! Don't quit!! The only way to fail is to stop!! Treat your business with the same professionalism you would if you had a real Jump Out Of Bed job!

How does your expertise help someone building a direct sales business?

If you haven't figured that out by now, then I guess I am totally whacked out!

What are the top 3 things you would recommend, based on your expertise, that accelerates business growth?

Well, three is not enough.... I have ONE or eight – Depending on how you look at it. Top ONE Thing I Recommend to Accelerate Growth - BUILD A Team!!! There are hundreds of team building tips for building an effective team but I will share eight simple ones that focus on the direct sales meeting. Meetings are a time to develop camaraderie, friendships and provide training. Meetings are a key component to growing an effective sales team.

#1 Get Your Team to Meetings

One of the best team building tips I can give you is to get your team to meetings. Whether it is digital meetings or live meetings, meeting makers definitely make more money and have a better chance of sticking with their home business. When you project the image to new and future consultants that all successful home business consultants DO go to meetings, then chances are they will. This starts long before they sign on the dotted line. Even before a new consultant signs up, some variation of the phrase "Meeting Makers Make More Money" should be included in your dialog.

Often times new or potential consultants ask: "Do I have to go to training meetings?" The leader often replies with an answer such as "No but it is recommended." The answer should be more like:
"You are in business for yourself so you can do what you want and all successful consultants do go to meetings! We meet the 4th Tuesday monthly and have a blast!" "You are in business for yourself but you are not alone. Meetings give you a chance to

connect with others and meeting makers always make more money!"

Get your team to meetings, online, offline and also national conferences and you will see your team retention go up, guaranteed! Put team incentives into place that market meetings to your team all year round!

#2 Tip for Effective Teams

Treat them like leaders from day one! Empower your team members from the beginning. When you run an effective meeting and delegate responsibility to your team they will begin to act like leaders long before they become leaders.

Don't wait for team members to express an interest in becoming a leader; treat them like a leader from day one and you will develop more leaders. Whether you are talking on the phone or in person, using words that indicate that they are leaders will plant seeds for the future.

#3 Team Building Tip: It Is Not All About You

Make sure that your meeting is all about the team. You are the last person that they want to hear from week after week – meeting after meeting! Tap into the team to educate and share... the leader should NOT be the main presenter!! Using a system of meeting planning that delegates the many parts of the meeting out to your team members, you will build a strong team who feel empowered by the process and want to keep coming back! Learn how to create engaging team meetings that people want to attend!

#4 Use Themes – Keep 'Em Guessing

When you keep your team guessing at what is happening next there will always be an air of excitement. Direct sales meeting themes that keep them guessing will keep them coming back for more!

#5 Train to Every Personality and Level

Left brain, right brain, logical, emotional.... we all think differently. Using a wide variety of training techniques allows you to teach to all the different personality types. Lectures, games, workshops, role play, etc. all teach to a different personality type. Learn more about training both sides of the brain with games.

#6 Teach The Basics at Every Meeting

Every team member is at a different level of knowledge within your organization. Chances are your business has 4-5 basic training points: recruiting, prospecting, sales, hostess coaching, etc. Teach each basic skill in a different manner at every single meeting. Short to-the-point training modules at every meeting will be better received than long tedious activities. Using the meeting planning template your company provides or one found on the Cash Flow Show make sure you hit every personality and every level of knowledge/skills within your team at every training session.

#7 Become A Leader Who Listens!

Empowering your team is all about keeping the focus on them! Remember that coaching a team or a consultant to success is about what they want. What are their goals? Do not push your goals on them but learn to become a good listener and empower them in meetings as well as individual coaching.

#8 Leverage Your Time

Take advantage of the systems already created for team building that leverage your time and make the most of your efforts! Utilizing systems of training that your company has created or those offered at the Cash Flow show will allow you to grow quickly. For example, the Super Starter Bookings Training for New Consultants teaches bookings to each team member as they join. The Direct Sales Recruiting University is designed to create a caring and sharing team. Both are affordable direct sales trainings that leverage your time!

Continue the Conversation with Deb Bixler:

 Deb Bixler, AKA The Bookings Queen, is the leading authority for home party plan business training. Using her party plan business as a tool to transition from the corporate world to entrepreneur, Deb has walked the walk and now teaches home party plan professionals how to do the same. She has been honored in the *Direct Selling Live Power 50,* the *Women Of Power awards and as the Direct Selling World Alliance* 2011 Speaker of The Year.

Below are the various ways that you can connect with Deb and learn more about what she has to offer.

- **Website:**
  www.CashFlowShow.com

- **Twitter:**
  www.twitter.com/DebBixler

- **Facebook:**
  www.facebook.com/DebBixler

MONICA RAMOS
Founder, MoneliCo Business Solutions

Tell us a little about yourself and how you were first introduced to the direct sales industry?

To be honest, I was never a fan of those "home product party" things. Being an introvert and very frugal about my time and money, the idea of hanging out with a bunch of strangers and spending money on products that I could probably find cheaper and get quicker at Walmart was NOT my idea of a good time. My friends knew better than to invite me to one of "those" parties. So, as you can probably imagine, it was quite surprising to not only myself, but everyone that knew me, when I joined my first direct sales company doing "those parties". Even more surprising was my enormous success.

I was first introduced to the direct sales industry in 2008 when my cousin invited me over for drinks and appetizers on a Thursday evening right after work. She sent me an invitation with a list of delicious food that would be sampled and even a few cocktails. I love to eat and drink so I said I would go. Shocking, I know. The best part was that it was right after work and on my way home. I got to sample all kinds of delicious food and ended up placing a $55 order. For me, at the time, that was a lot of money.

During the party consultant's presentation, which she made look really easy by using script cards, I was surprised to hear that this was her first show. As I was sampling the food and flipping through the catalog, I thought to myself, "I can do this." I had just bought my first home and could really use the extra income. I asked her a bunch of questions about the business but she didn't seem too eager to sign me up. I ended up going online a few days later and signing myself up under her.

That business kept me afloat and I was able to pay my new mortgage for a few months. Then everything changed when there was a statewide furlough and my paycheck was cut by $800 a month. People had to drastically adjust their spending and habits to survive this. The problem was that everything they were all doing—cutting back on cable, not eating out, getting part-time jobs—I had already done to be able to go from paying $600 a month rent to a $1600 mortgage payment. We even pulled our oldest out of private school to afford that house. Had I known the furlough was coming I would have never bought that house.

To keep my home and be able to feed my children, I worked my business harder and rented out the downstairs bedroom in my home, cramming my 3 children together upstairs. Two years of that left me depressed, exhausted, and over $30,000 in credit card debt. I couldn't believe that I was working so hard and feeling like I was drowning. Then a friend of mine approached me at work one day and told me about this new direct selling company and invited me to her launch party. The product was intriguing but I was broke, so I told her I would be there for support but that I could not buy anything.

When I arrived at her party I was shocked to see so many women fighting over this new product and freely handing over their credit cards. Even I made a purchase. What's an extra $100 of debt when you're drowning in it? I saw a demand for a unique product and knew this would be an easy product to sell. After learning that my friend made over $800 in commission in one afternoon, I knew this was the opportunity that could change my life.

After returning home to share my excitement with my husband (who is much more frugal than I am) I was surprised by how supportive he was about the business. The company was brand new and the "starter kit" was a hefty $1,500 investment so it was a big chance I took, but I knew this was going to be ticket out of debt, depression, and exhaustion. With tax season around the corner I took a leap of faith and maxed out my last credit card that had any wiggle room left and started my new journey. I made more on my first show than I was averaging in a month with my first direct sales company. Six weeks later I had completely made back my initial investment. After my first year I was able to pay off $14,000 of credit card debt, purchase a new car (I had been borrowing from my in-laws to do my parties), and no longer needed to rent out the room in my house and my kids finally had their own rooms. I had earned my first all-inclusive tropical vacation for two and was feeling much better about my future. Around this time the company had transitioned into the party plan model and I was able to start building a team. Within 16 months I had rank advanced 6 times and found myself at the top of the compensation plan with the fastest growing team in the company, a collection of trophies and award certificates, and had just earned my third all expenses paid vacation. So I did what I never thought I'd be able to do. I quit my full time job and was able to run a profitable business I enjoyed from home and spend more time with my family.

And to think it all started with drinks and appetizers. You never know whose life you can change by inviting them to a party or sharing your business opportunity. Sometimes your most successful team member turns out to be the one you least expected.

Share with us what your business is and why you focus on supporting the direct sales industry?

I have recently transitioned out of the direct sales industry as a field representative to focus on helping others achieve success as a business coach and social media trainer. Before entering the direct sales world, I had a very small, part-time business helping people develop their web presence. I built websites, blog sites, designed logos, and created social media business pages for friends, family, and local business owners who were not tech savvy. When I incorporated that knowledge into my direct sales business I discovered a passion for training, especially in internet marketing and social media. I had packaged many training programs for my team and even built an entire interactive team website to host them on electronically. I had a training program for everything from mindset to leadership to Facebook. When team leaders from other companies started to reach out to me for help I realized I had an opportunity to help more people and I decided to use my experience as a successful leader to create the foundation for the next chapter in my business career. I now coach and train small business owners, who are made up mostly of direct sellers, on how to market their businesses effectively online, support their team members for continued growth, and establish a mindset for accelerated success.

What is your favorite thing about the direct sales industry?

My favorite thing about this industry is the low entry barrier. Where else can you start a business for less than $200? It's the perfect entry point for someone with an entrepreneurial spirit who doesn't have the financial backing to build a business from scratch. It's a gateway industry. I've learned so much about relationship marketing, interpersonal communication, team building, leadership, goal setting, life-work balance, and the incredible power of a positive mindset from all the failures and successes I've experienced in this industry.

What is the most rewarding aspect of working with Direct Sales entrepreneurs?

I love working with positive, passionate people and those are exactly the kind of people that this industry breeds. The direct sales industry offers limitless opportunity for growth and success. Often times I work with direct sellers who understand that but have trouble picturing what success looks like for them and how to get there. Everyone is successful at something. I enjoy helping my clients to discover what that is for themselves and helping them feel positive about the direction their headed. There is great joy in watching someone transition into their own version of success.

What is your definition of a successful direct sales entrepreneur?

This is different for everyone. When working with clients who feel stuck or unmotivated I usually ask them to remember the reason they joined. What was so appealing about this opportunity? Often times, the problem is that what they thought they would get out of it (more time, more money, more fun) has gotten lost along the way. I will ask a client to close her eyes and picture her ideal day as business owner. Where do you live? Do you work your business from home or out of the home? What does your office look like? What time do you get up in the morning? What's the first thing you do? How many hours per day are you working on your business? How many days a week? How much money are you making? Once they have this clear picture painted in their mind, I ask them how many of the things on their current "to do" list are supporting that vision. I then give them permission to delete or delegate anything on that list that is not supporting the life they are working on creating. Success is a different picture for everyone. I started my direct sales business to get out of debt and have more time with my family with less stress about money. I didn't get rich from my direct selling business, but I sure was successful!

What do you consider great characteristics of successful entrepreneurs?

A positive mindset and the belief in your ability to achieve your version of success; being intentional in your actions and decisions; recognizing your weaknesses and incorporating the support of a well-balanced team; making time for self-care and non-business related fun, and passion—you've got to really love what you do.

What advice would you give someone who is ready to take their business to the next level?

If you want to grow a team and up your sponsoring game, you have to make it look easy so that others can see themselves doing what you do. Don't go overboard with your party presentation. You should be able to get everything into your hostess's house in one trip from the car. Your set up should only take 10 to 20 minutes and your presentation should be between 30 and 45 minutes. You want your hostess and her guests to be able to picture themselves doing what you do. The consultant at very first party I attended was reading script cards and I thought to myself, "That looks easy. I could do this!" And you know how that story went.

To increase bookings, tell your hostess to keep the refreshments simple—something savory, something sweet, and something wet. Guests notice these things and if it looks like hosting a party is a lot of work or will cost a lot of money, they're not going to be volunteering any time soon.

Some of my clients tell me they like having their party orders shipped to them first so they can assemble them with decorative packaging, add a thank you note, and deliver them in person. I guarantee your hostesses and customers will love you for this, but they will most likely not be in any hurry to join your team and do what you do.

The same goes for training your team. If you have a lot of products in your display that are not included in the normal starter kit, your team will think they have to invest in all that extra stuff too. You want your team making money when they start, not spending it. I don't believe in telling people they have to spend money to make money. I say make money with what you got (your starter kit should be enough), then use some of the money you make to invest in products and services that will help you make more money and support the growth of your business.

If you answer emails, texts, and Facebook messages from your team at all hours of the night or put on elaborate meetings with expensive giveaways, your team is going to think that they have to do all that to be as successful as you. A great mentor once asked me, "Does your team want your job? And can they do your job?" If you are posting to your Facebook group at 2 in the morning, they are going to think you never sleep. Set office hours and model the behavior you want to foster. No need to re-invent the wheel and create elaborate training materials if the home office has a good system in place. Use what is available. If the corporate office does not have something in place, look for trainers, speakers, and coaches whose systems and training packages have worked for you, and share those resources with your team. If the training material is out there somewhere, don't recreate it, just show your team where to get it.

What are some of the big AH-HAs you have seen entrepreneurs experience that then propel them to the next level?

One of the biggest ah-ha moments I had was when I stopped giving out my contact information and leaving brochures and business cards everywhere hoping someone would call, email, or place an order on my site. I decided it was time to take control of my business and stop leaving it to chance. I trained my team and teach my clients to do the same. Whenever you meet someone who is interested in learning more about your business or the products you offer, ask them for *their* contact information. I usually say, "As much as I'd love to take your money and sell these to you at full price, you can actually get them cheaper through our special programs and promotions. Give me your email [or you can ask for a phone number or both] and I'll send you some more info about our specials, including how you can get free products. I'll also send you a coupon for an additional 10% off your first order."

If I have an upcoming open house or I'm planning an inventory sale, I would say, "You know a new collection comes out every month. Do you live around here? I do a big inventory clearance about 3 times a year and my next one is this weekend. I've got to make room for all the new stuff coming out so I'm having a big blow out my retired inventory. The new line will be on display and available to order too. Would you like me to send you a flyer and my inventory list?"

My favorite one is, "Oh, man, I'm fresh out of catalogs, but I have new ones arriving tomorrow. Give me your info and I'll send you one." At one point I stopped ordering business cards so I could use the fact that I didn't have any on me to collect contact information to follow up later.

Most people won't refuse the opportunity to look over information and decide for themselves if they want to purchase. By presenting it this way they feel in control about whether they decide to buy full price, at a discount, or explore the many opportunities my business has to offer.

The important thing is that you actually follow up. And don't just send a catalog. Include promotional material about any specials you have, events coming that they can attend, the benefits of hosting a party, and an opportunity brochure about the business. Put these contacts on your email list and send updates regularly, at least once a month.

Too many times direct sellers are quick to hand out their business cards to every person who says they're interested and then they never hear from those people. It doesn't mean they weren't really interested. They probably got busy and forgot or lost your information. Or even worse, they ran into another consultant selling your same product and instead of giving them her business card (like you did) she got theirs and now has them her email list.

I can't tell you how many times I think to myself, "I really need to order more _____" or "I'm running low on _____. I wonder if that lady still sells this stuff. What was her name again?" Or maybe I do know her name, and I have her number in my phone, but I get busy and forget to call. Then I'm at a vendor event and some other consultant is there selling the exact product I need. Had the representative that I originally purchased from kept in regular contact with I would have purchased from her again.

It's imperative that you take control of your business by building and nurturing your list of leads and customers. Your success depends on it. Many of my team members and clients have reported that after implementing this single change their business began to flourish.

What have direct selling entrepreneurs shared with you that they wish they had known when they started?

New leaders often report that they don't want to come off bossy or pushy so they give their new team members the freedom to work as little or as much as they want. I fell victim to this too. I was a self-starter and never felt I needed help from my upline or maybe I just didn't want to feel like I had a boss. So I assumed that's how everyone felt too. After all, people go into business for themselves so that they can do it their way. Or so I thought. I later learned that by not getting my team off to great start I was doing them a disservice. I was setting them up for failure.

I began offering every new team member I sponsored the opportunity to have a thriving business within their first 90 days. I let them know that if they could commit to following my proven success plan for their first 90 days, they were free to run their business however they wanted after that. If they only want to sell online or only do vendor events after the 90 days, that was fine with me. I was ok with it because I knew something they didn't. By setting up and following a successful business plan from day 1 they ended up on day 90 with money in their pockets, a calendar full of bookings, and some had even started building a team and promoting to leadership levels. By that point there was no going back. They knew what it took to be successful because they had done it.

Many times when a new direct seller is not successful in her first few months, she feels resentment towards her sponsor. In some way her sponsor made her think she could do this, that it would be easy, or that the product "sells itself" and the money would just come rolling in. When she is not successful, she can feel somewhat cheated. It doesn't happen all the time, but it happens. When you commit to the success of your new team members from the beginning, they never feel tricked, they have a successful business to brag about, and will more than likely continue the same process with their new team members.

Not everyone will be committed and that's ok. Offer your help to every new team member and work with ones who accept. It's not your job to make them do the work, all you need to do is offer the opportunity. Don't let the fear of coming off pushy or bossy make you selfish. You know how good of an opportunity this is and you know how to run a successful business. Share that knowledge with everyone on your team.

What do you see direct sales leaders do to keep motivated and encouraging of their team when things aren't going right?

Mindset is everything. It's important to focus on what's going right and celebrate even the small successes. When items in your catalog are selling out before the season is over, don't blame the company for not forecasting the demand. Instead, teach your team to spin it in a way that has them focusing on how popular and in demand your products are. Would you rather have a catalog full of items no one wants or products so popular that you have to encourage your customer to order now before they're gone.

When you have a party at the end of the month in a low-income neighborhood do you go in thinking no one is going to buy because they don't have money? Or do you notice how nicely everyone is dressed, that they all have smart phones, and the elaborate spread of food and beverages the hostess has laid out and think these people have money and like to spend it?

If no one shows up for your hostess' party use that opportunity to go through the catalog together and provide an intimate shopping experience for her. Have her call up a few friends and see if they want to place an online order. Or maybe help her with gift ideas for any upcoming holidays or birthdays. When you leave feel good knowing that you were in the right place at the right time and your professionalism made such an impression to the hostess that perhaps she is going to hustle up some orders or maybe even decide to join your team and re-invite everyone to her launch.

You've got to see the opportunity in every situation and know that it's okay to have off days or even really slow months. That doesn't mean things will stay that way. We all started at zero when we joined and we have the tools and support to help us get to where we want to be. Encourage your team to work together to see possibilities and solutions, not problems. You will always find what you are looking for, so make sure you're looking for the good stuff. Every time and in every situation.

What are the mistakes you have seen leaders make that stifle the growth of their teams?

One mistake I see too often is sponsoring the wrong person at the wrong time. Sometimes we see the business as a good fit for someone but they may not be ready. If you have to do a lot of convincing to get them signed up, you will most likely have to put in a lot of effort to keep them motivated to stay, or worse, hold their hand every step of the way. Sponsor people who want to work the business by empowering them from the beginning instead of enabling them. A good example of enabling instead of empowering is when you offer to pay for all or part of a prospect's starter kit. You may think you are helping them get started with their business but you are actually hindering their chance at real success. A prospective team member that cannot afford your starter kit but sees the opportunity as an investment will find a way to pay for it, and in doing so will empower herself to make it work. When you don't have to work as hard for something, you don't perceive it as valuable.

When training and developing your team you should seek to create a culture that continues to foster empowerment. Instead of answering a question over and over again I would tell my team where to find the answer themselves. Over time they would ask less and less because they knew what I was going to say. This is not to say that I would not provide help when my team reached out to me, but if the answer was something I knew they did not need me to help them figure out, like how much a Director makes on their first, I would respond by asking if they had a copy of the comp plan and if they knew where get one. I can show my team where to download our comp plan from the back office but I'm not going to read it for them. If you want go getters on your team you have to stop enabling them to be the opposite.

What are the biggest surprises/hurdles entrepreneurs face once they become leaders?

The biggest obstacles I find that the newest leaders (and seasoned leaders too) face is finding a manageable balance between maintaining their personal business, growing a team, and developing leaders within their team. Many leaders have complained that they are spending too much time on working with and training their team that their personal business begins to suffer.

This is usually the result of creating training that doesn't need to be created, usually because the home office has sufficient training in place or there are external resources that can be leveraged to benefit everyone. Often times your company has great training programs, resources, and systems in place so there's no sense in reinventing the wheel, but if your company does not yet offer this support (maybe they are new), there are a lot of well-known trainers in this industry who offer incredible training programs for direct sellers. If you find a great resource that is already created, share it with your team.

I also see leaders get discouraged when they get so good at sponsoring that the bookings on their calendar keep disappearing because their hostesses become their team members and those customers and potential booking leads become the new team members' contacts. You've got to look at this in a positive light. This was my problem when I was growing my team. I had to keep rebuilding my personal business each month as I grew my team, but I looked at it as an opportunity to keep from getting out of practice. I was better equipped to train my team on how to get bookings and generate new leads because it was something I had to keep doing in my own business.

What is the one key piece of advice you have given to the leaders you coach that has proven the most successful?

Model the behavior you want to see. Your team looks up to you and they are always watching. If you want your team to remain positive in difficult situations, you must not get into conversations (online or in person) that breed negativity. If you want your team holding 4 to 6 parties a month you must also be holding parties regularly. If you want to have a team of go-getters and self-starters who are not so busy working with their teams that their own businesses suffer, then teach them how to come up with their own solutions instead of just answering every question they have.

If you were standing in front of 200 new field members who just joined a direct sales company what 3 things would you share?

Define your priorities. Put the 5 F's first: Family, Faith, Fitness/Food, Finances, and Fun. If you're not happy, healthy, and able to love and support your family, you won't be successful in business. Pull out your calendar and put the important things in first. This should include your kids' activities, date nights, self-care appointments, family outings or vacations, and time you need to commit to your regular job if you are not doing this business full time. Then, schedule in your bookings, meetings, and training events related to your business.

Collect contact information from each person that shows an interest in your products or business. Don't leave the success of your business up to others. When you do hand out marketing materials (catalog, flyers, business cards, etc.) include a call to action that gives them a reason to contact you instead of the next consultant in your company that they meet. An effective yet simple call to action to include on your promotional materials is "Email me at _____ for 15% off your first order!"

Don't try to do it alone. Attend your monthly training meetings and annual conventions, interact with and learn from other consultants in Facebook groups or other networking forums, and ask for help when you need it. When you see others succeeding in this business ask them for their best tips. The most successful direct sellers are always willing to share their best tips.

Find someone who is already where you want to be in this business and take their advice.

What have you learned about yourself while working with top leaders in the direct sales industry?

I've learned that my way is not always the best way. By surrounding myself with experienced and positive people I have learned to be more open to new ways of doing the same old things. I've learned to celebrate the successes of others and not compare my beginning to someone else's middle. Comparison kills contentment and your success is dependent on how successful you feel. It's a lot more fun to live your life your way, on your terms, in a way that works best for you. Keep a running list of your small successes and celebrate and honor them every chance you get. When you see others achieving the goals you set out for yourself let it inspire you and motivate you to keep going. After all, if they can do it, you know it's possible.

How does your expertise help someone building a direct sales business?

As a social media trainer, I try to remind my clients that people generally go online for two reasons: to learn something or to be entertained. Social Media is no different, except that there is a third reason added: to socialize with their friends. Direct sellers using social media for business need to understand that and they need to think more like a user, and less like a marketer. There is too much promotion and too many "buy my stuff" or "help me earn..." posts out there and they give the direct selling industry a bad name. If you wouldn't talk to your friends using those words, don't post them on social media. People don't like to be sold to, but they love to discover. Give them that education, entertainment, and the social relationships they go online looking for and you will be much more successful in your marketing efforts. Provide value and be a resource people respect and trust. Once you develop that rapport you'll find the sales come naturally, and most often happen offline. Social media is the lead generation and relationship building tool, not the sales tool. The people who need your products and services will want to buy from you, and you'll feel better about yourself for providing them with what they need as opposed to trying to convince them they need what you offer. Stop posting so many promotional posts and let your audience learn a little more about the person behind the business. If you're business has allowed you to spend more time with your family, post about the kinds of things you are doing with this freedom. People do business with people. They will be more open to doing business with you if they feel they can relate you.

What are the top 3 things you would recommend, based on your expertise, that accelerates business growth?

Develop and nurture a positive mindset and create a daily habit of focusing only on what is going right. You will get more of what you focus your attention on.

Your success is dependent on how successful you feel. Celebrate all your successes, even the small ones, so you feel good. That will lead to more successes. Believe in your ability to achieve the goals you have set for yourself. Know it with so much certainty that obstacles become games you play for fun along the journey.

Continue the Conversation with Monica Ramos:

 Monica Ramos is a wife, mother, and entrepreneur who believes life is meant to be fun and easy. She is a certified Social Media Trainer and Brain Coach and considers herself a life-long learner with an unquenchable thirst for knowledge. Monica is fascinated by the unlimited powers of the mind and how our thoughts and beliefs can create the lives we dream of. She is passionate about helping people see the positive in any situation and credits most, if not all, of her success to her beliefs—in her products, in her company, in her team, and in herself. Monica is dedicated to helping her clients grow their businesses and enrich their lives by teaching them to honor their true desires, do what feels good, and follow the path of least resistance. When you get your mindset right first, your actions become aligned and intentional, and seem almost effortless, creating the perfect recipe for success in life and business.

Below are the various ways that you can connect with Monica and learn more about what she has to offer.

- **Website:**
  www.monicaramos.tv

- **Twitter:**
  www.twitter.com/monicaramostv

- **Facebook:**
  www.facebook.com/monicaramostv

KAREN CLARK
Founder, My Business Presence

Tell us a little about yourself and how you were first introduced to the direct sales industry?

Before direct sales, I was living in Pensacola, Florida and married to my high school sweetheart who had joined the Navy. I had been a teacher for a few years out of college but at that time I was staying home with my 2 young daughters who were about 1 and 4. I was the typical mom that planned on only taking a year off after the baby and then going back to work but I just couldn't leave them. My husband was pressuring me to go back to work but I just couldn't. I really didn't have a backup plan and we needed my income. I wasn't really looking to do direct sales, but I knew I'd need to make an income to contribute to my family. However, I was kind of putting it off as long as possible.

I was invited to a party but couldn't attend so I booked my own. The response was incredible and I ended up joining! It took off like crazy, despite me not having any experience in direct sales. Unfortunately, we were transferred to Washington State and I found myself scrambling to keep up the momentum and I turned to the internet. I learned to start building my online presence for my business, with the blessing of the company, and that was key to my early success. I began blogging, hand-coding web pages and learning all about SEO while exploring various forums for moms, teachers and military families. I joined e-groups and bulletin boards, hung out in work at home mom chat rooms and placed online classified ads.

I was excited to be able to use the internet to keep in touch with my friends and customers in Florida while also starting to meet new people in my new state of Washington. What I wasn't expecting was to start building teams all around the USA in the process. It turns out that many people, even back then, turned to the internet looking for ways to make money. I quickly began building teams in states where our company had no presence, while at the same time continuing to build my offline in-home party business. I easily fell in love with direct sales and especially leading my team both long distance and local.

Share with us what your business is and why you focus on supporting the direct sales industry?

After 12 years with that company, moving up in leadership and into a corporate position, I found myself at a crossroads. Since I had experienced early success with internet marketing and direct sales, it was a natural transition for me to begin teaching others how to market themselves online. After just a few months experimenting with that locally, it was clear that was a much needed service. At first, I thought it would be best for me to do social media management for others so I did a little of that while also holding workshops and doing some one on one coaching. I was not working much within the direct sales arena at first and something always felt like it was missing. When I finally realized that where I belonged was in direct sales but as a trainer, it was as if everything fell into place for me to begin this second career.

My primary business now is corporate consulting and speaking at conferences. I have a variety of training materials and courses I offer to audience members or individuals who I meet in other ways. My focus is almost all on those in direct sales because not only do I speak the language, but I love the industry! Since going out on my own in 2009 I have been on a mission to educate more and more direct sellers on how we can uplift the reputation of direct sales through our behavior in social media. We already have a little bit of an uphill battle when we try to explain to people what it is that we do. Some people don't understand it or there's a negative stigma associated with home-based businesses in some circles. With the popularity of social media combined with direct sales - the original social network - there's no reason why we can't show the world how amazing and life-changing this industry truly is while working our businesses ethically and effectively,

What is your favorite thing about the direct sales industry?

I honestly LOVE home parties and I love the products. I am a big direct sales supporter and have been known to book home parties for different companies every month of the year! No matter what I do in my life I know I will be holding home parties because they give me a way to connect with friends and family, to learn about new products and ideas, and to earn some free products. I am the ideal hostess because I am SO into it! People who say home parties are going to the wayside are wrong. I love them. I find that most direct sales companies' products are far superior to those you can buy in the stores, and of course we know the customer service is unparalleled. I'm a big fan of direct sales!

What is the most rewarding aspect of working with direct sales entrepreneurs?

For me the biggest reward comes with empowering people to do things they either never thought that they could, or were too intimidated to try. Working primarily with a technology focus, I run into this often, especially in the very high-touch person-to-person business of direct sales. There is nothing more satisfying for me than to meet a seasoned leader who has been wildly successful in her business but feels completely inadequate and deflated when it comes to technology. Knowing that she must learn how to address it in order to keep up with her team and new developments in the industry, she receives coaching or takes one of my courses. Due to the way that I teach she finally gets it!

Having been a teacher I understand how to take complex topics such as technology and break them down into easy to understand methods so that everyone, regardless of skill level, feels comfortable and able to implement. Being able to hear from a seasoned yet intimidated leader, who is now able to have personal success online, teach her team new skills, and feel like "Wonder Woman" in the process, is priceless! For most of us in the industry we understand that a big part of what we get out of it is the personal growth and development. Being able to have a hand in helping someone accomplish something that once felt overwhelming is amazing!

What is your definition of a successful direct sales entrepreneur?

Success in direct sales is not a dollar figure, a bonus or a number in your downline. It isn't the awards you receive on stage; the kudos you receive from the company or your upline leader. It isn't how many incentives you've earned or the free car sitting in your garage. I feel that success in direct sales has more to do with who you have become in the process of achieving all that you have, whether it's your first year or your 40th.

There is a book by Catherine Ponder, The Dynamic Laws of Prosperity, in which she says that you are prosperous to the degree that you are experiencing peace, health, happiness and plenty in your life and I truly believe that. In fact, I have it printed out and posted on the wall in my office. Success is a combination of not just material achievements through the years but of also balancing your time with self-care, relationships, fun, and personal growth.

Having been in the field as a top leader and training leaders through my corporate position and now as a consultant, I have seen many "successful" direct sellers sacrifice their health, their relationships, and their inner peace for their businesses. I say, what good is it to be making a large sum of money or earn every trip if you aren't getting enough sleep, aren't able to spend time with those you love, or are always stressed out? It is vital in my opinion that as direct sellers grow their businesses, they consider the rest of their lives as equally important and set personal goals alongside their business goals.

Set goals to have monthly date nights with your spouse. Set a goal to be completely present during time spent with your children. Set a goal to have a regular morning routine including exercise or a nighttime routine of reading just for fun.

What are your insights about the direct selling industry that will best help people build a strong business?

Direct sales is all about the people and that is where your focus should be. We love our products, we love our prizes, but without relationships we have nothing. Direct sales, like social media, is about connecting with people, not collecting people. In order to build a strong and long lasting business with customers and teams who will be loyal to you, you have got to put people first.

When it comes to customers, this means personalizing your approach and getting to know them. Think of your customers as your friends and behave accordingly. When it comes to social media, don't forget that those are people on the other end of the computer. Get to know them, ask them questions, talk to them as if making the sale is the last thing on your mind. This is what builds loyalty, when people know you sincerely care whether or not they ever do business with you. Then when they see that you do have something to offer them, they are much more likely to act on it by purchasing or sharing it with their friends.

As a leader, think about how to build an even stronger bond with those on your team, instead of thinking of how they can help you meet your minimums, earn the next trip, or advance to the next rank. Build your relationships. Start a private Facebook group where you encourage them every day and begin to build community among your team. Make personal phone calls or start personal chats, just to check in with people about their lives, not to ask if they've placed all their orders yet. Send your team members a card in the mail, a small gift, or a random "This made me think of you" message online. There is nothing more precious to a home based business person than to be noticed by the person they look up to in their company and that is you!

Unfortunately for many they focus on the numbers, or the product, and spend more time getting ready to sell than they do on developing relationships. This is one way I think the direct sales industry is unique from other businesses where you rely more on yourself and your own skills, or from a traditional job where you are more task-oriented. When someone in direct sales gets the difference, it shows in their results because building those relationships is what matters most.

What advice would you give someone who is ready to take their business to the next level?

Since I come from a place of making sure everyone is maximizing their opportunities to build their businesses online as well as offline, I would offer the advice to make sure whichever your favorite social media tool is, that it is set up correctly and you are utilizing all its features. I have never been one to suggest that every entrepreneur be present on all of the social media sites but instead to choose one that is their favorite and to develop systems to use it as best they can until it is like a well-oiled machine before going on to add another platform.

For example:

- Create a dedicated business page to market your business if you aren't already.
- Start a closed group to support your team.
- Check that your About tab is fully filled out with lots of verbiage about your product lines, hosting parties, and business opportunity. Share your why story.
- Conduct an opportunity call but use a Facebook event to promote it. Boost the event (if your company allows) to targeted groups or email lists.

What is the best description of the relationship between a field member and their corporate office?

I have always seen representatives and the home office as partners who are dependent on each other. Two halves of a whole. Without field representatives the company could not grow. Without home office support, the representatives would not be able to do their jobs. When both parties see the relationship as a partnership, it is easier to truly listen to each others' needs and respects each others' requests.

In my social media marketing training one of the first things I mention is for consultants to check and double check their corporate policies and procedures when it comes to social media and internet marketing. When I consult with companies, one of the first requests I have is to read their social media policies and procedures so that I can support them in my training. This is also so that I can make suggestions if the P&P isn't quite up to date or as thorough as needed.

It is important for both parties to understand the needs of the other. For example, a home office who understands the field's need to feel empowered to make much of their own choices when it comes to how they run their business will create policies that may be a little more open to leaving room for creativity. When the field understands that building a scalable brand that stands the test of time relies on consistent messaging and images that reflect the company culture, they are more accepting of some of the restrictions the company may need to place on their creativity. The best situation is when a win-win can be created among everyone and the key to that is listening with an open mind and truly collaborating, as true partners would.

Consistency and reproducible are terms often used by direct sales leaders. What are some of the most successful systems you have seen used by top leaders?

With regard to social media for leaders, many create private groups where they can build community among their teams. Using a private group such as those on Facebook can also give you a platform to address questions and offer your own training. To encourage interaction and community support in your team group, one system I love is having a theme for something you post on each day of the week. Some examples might be:

- Monday: Motivation, or Money Matters, or Movie (video)
- Tuesday: Tip, or Team Building, or Time Management
- Wednesday: Wacky, or Wonderful (recognition)
- Thursday: Thoughts (quotes), or Thankful Friday: Fun, or Freedom, or Fast Facts, or Flashback

This can help you decide what to post each day and keep conversations going. Another thing that works well is to have a Question of the Week where you encourage everyone to chime in about something. Posting a Product of the Week and sharing lesser-known facts or tips is great too, and helps newer members develop their product knowledge. Another idea is to post a Dilemma of the Day in a "what would you do?" type of scenario. Let your team brainstorm together how to handle tough situations or objections.

As your team begins to grow and you develop leaders under you, they will find it easy to create their own team groups and do the same. Making leadership as simple as possible is key to developing a larger organization.

What have direct selling entrepreneurs shared with you that they wish they had known when they started?

Over and over I have heard that people wished they paid more attention to their spending earlier in their business. It is easy to become lured into purchasing unnecessary supplies, extra giveaways, fancy packaging, inventory and team gifts before you have the business profit to justify it. Investing in expensive outside coaching, tools and trainings is another way that consultants cut into their profits. This isn't necessary especially when you are new. One of the best benefits of joining direct sales is that your company provides everything you need to get started with very little additional expenses needed.

Don't try to get so creative that you are spending all of your profits on things that might be fun but really don't bring you more success. Not only will you start to feel like you aren't making enough money in your business to keep it going, but spending too much is something that your team will either copy and also feel unsuccessful or frustrated, or that prospects may see and decide not to join because it doesn't seem practical. I know someone who used to offer Coach purses to her new team members. Knowing how much in sales it would require to offset that expense, it seems outrageous. But what's more is that people considering joining the business would be scared away because as we know, your team will do what you do (whether you want them to or not!)

Track your income and expenses on a monthly or weekly basis. Create a budget for supplies and other categories you may truly need, and stick to it. As your business becomes more profitable your budget can increase and you can start setting aside real profits for the future.

What is a characteristic that you have seen that makes you immediately recognize a future leader?

It all comes back to relationships. When I see someone who truly is present with people and cares, I see a leader. When they are open to learning and being coached by others while at the same time love teaching and coaching, they would be a great leader. When I became a leader it was not intentional. In fact, I think that in many cases in direct sales, leaders develop accidentally in a sense, not intentionally. It is because of their ability to truly connect with people that attracts others to the business and it often just happens organically. People see who you are as a person and want that for themselves, too! Next thing you know, you're a leader!

What are the mistakes you have seen leaders make that stifle the growth of their teams?

Unfortunately, some leaders forget that each and every individual on their team has a story of their own. They have their own struggles and their own joys. Their own priorities and their own motivation for doing the business. Not every person will work at the pace that you want, so equip them with the tools they need, and make room for them to use them at the pace that works with their own lives.

When leaders become more like the ringleader cracking the whip and pressuring people to do things, it comes across as negative and demanding instead of gracious and generous. This can cause people to lose interest in the business. Remember to model positivity whenever you can, but also don't forget your humanity and remain sensitive to the differences you'll find on your team. Not everyone will be your rock star, but everyone deserves a chance to reach for their own goals.

What is the best investment you have seen direct sales entrepreneurs make in themselves?

I see investments as something you put in, to get something even greater out. For me, there is no greater investment than time with your family. Putting in presence, true presence, with your family today, will pay off big dividends in the future. Whether it is with your children, small or grown, your spouse or significant other, your own parents, siblings or cousins, the time you invest in relationships always pays off.

Too often I meet entrepreneurs who get so caught up in the "hustle" of building their businesses that they don't even realize their family members miss them. Children will never see the world through the same eyes tomorrow as they do today. We can't get that time back. Our adult parents' days are limited and it means so much to them when we take time out and give them a call to say hello, or meet them for lunch. Being present with the people who are important to you–truly present with the smart phones put away–is, to me, the best path to a "rich" life!

If you were standing in front of 200 new field members who just joined a direct sales company what 3 things would you share?

1. Know that although you may have joined this business for a variety of reasons, you're going to want to stay because of the people!
2. Always be learning. Attend your company and leaders' trainings and attend your meetings and conferences. Read the advice of others who have found success and learn from them.
3. Don't reinvent the wheel. Success is within your reach and honestly it's not rocket science. Anyone can go straight to the top if they want to. Just do the work.

What have you learned about yourself while working with top leaders in the direct sales industry?

I have gotten so many great ideas from top leaders! Most important is to create duplicable systems that work. Working with leaders has shown me just how important this is and I've applied that to my own business as well as in my training. If you cannot create a system that can be duplicated by yourself as well as your team members at any level, you will grow more slowly and find yourself frustrated and asking yourself, "Why can't they all just be like me?" If you find yourself asking that question, it's because what you are doing is not duplicable enough for them to follow your lead.

How does your expertise help someone building a direct sales business?

Although not a replacement for traditional marketing methods such as in-home parties, vendor events or one on one meetings, social media can be a powerful additional marketing avenue for your business when done correctly and consistently. It can enable you to meet people in new areas where you or your company may not ever had access as they discover you through their own friends or via the search engines. It can help you service your customers on a regular basis even more often than if you only relied on the telephone because so many people do not pick up these days but they do go on social media.

If you are a leader, using social media can help you connect with your team all over the country or the world and offer training, support and coaching so that your team can grow stronger and become a connected community regardless of location.

What are the top 3 things you would recommend, based on your expertise, that accelerates business growth?

1.) As excited as you are about your new business and its products, social media marketing is not about telling your friends and family to buy your products or book a party in every post. Take the time to think about what your connections would appreciate learning about whether they ever buy or book from you and post from a place of being in service to them. I recommend a proportion of about 90% non-promotional posts to 10% of your posts being about your product, booking, or income opportunity. If you like, add in a post about yourself or something casual and fun once in a while, too! This proportion helps build trust and rapport which creates a loyal following.

2.) Consistency in posting to social media, especially Facebook, is important. In order to be visible create a daily routine of commenting on a few others' posts, posting something new yourself, and replying to comments. I call this Social Media CPR: Comment, Post, Reply. It's easy to do in about 15 or 20 minutes per day on a regular basis.

3.) Keep your social media posts simple and leverage the resources your home office supplies. There is no need for you to become an expert graphic designer or to erect a video production studio in your garage! Your company has many images, videos and marketing copy that can be shared to your networks when promoting your product and opportunity. Save yourself the time and aggravation so that you have more time to personalize your message and connect with people. Add your own caption so that the expertise is brought to you, but leverage your home office images and videos whenever you can. They are usually well thought out and great tools for your marketing!

Continue the Conversation with Karen Clark

 A pioneer in using social media for direct sales, Karen Clark has been practicing ethical and effective Internet Marketing since 1998. While a field Leader, Karen was an innovator in bringing the company to the Internet and expanding the sales force by combining traditional party plan marketing with online relationship building. Since 2009 she has been consulting and training with various companies, promoting the use of social media marketing for connecting people, not collecting people.

Below are the various ways that you can connect with Karen and learn more about what she has to offer.

- **Website:**
  www.mybusinesspresence.com

- **Twitter:**
  www.twitter.com/mybizpresence

- **Facebook:**
  www.facebook.com/mybusinesspresence

TERESA GARRISON
Founder, The Success Factory

Tell us a little about yourself and how you were first introduced to the direct sales industry?

I am a true southern girl. I was raised in North Carolina and moved to Texas with my family in my twenties where I met my wonderful husband, David. We have been married for 24 years and I am so honored to have such a loving, strong man who believes in me and supports me in everything I do.

Thanks to direct sales, David and I spent the first 20 years of our marriage traveling all over the world by attending conferences, trainings and best of all free travel earned through incentive trips. Some of our favorite trips have been Hong Kong, Maui, Vienna, Scotland and Paris. I love the fact I joined direct sales and it rewarded me with being able to see the world! Recently we have been blessed to begin a new journey in our lives and have started a family. In 2011, we adopted our son Beckett. In March of 2015, David, Beckett and I traveled to China and brought home our daughter, Piper. These two little ones bring constant joy, chaos, laughter, craziness and fun to our home. Who thought at this point in our lives when most people are becoming empty nesters that we would be changing diapers? It is keeping us young and believe me we love every single second of it!

So how did I end up in direct sales? After David and I were married, I assumed our next step should be to buy a new house. However, David reminded me that we were broke newlyweds and could not afford a house yet. One day I was out with my mom and said "Let's just check out this neighborhood" and we happened to pass a lady putting a *For Sale* sign in her front yard. "Let's just see if she will show us the house mom". One hour later I had negotiated a lease on the house for six months until we could come up with the down payment. Then I had to tell my husband. And yes, I am still married to that same man! We moved in three weeks later. With just six months to come up with the down payment, we both agreed to get part time jobs. David is a landscape architect so he could do design work on the side. I had a very demanding full time job in the corporate world so I thought I would check out the shopping center down the street for a job in retail. David wasn't convinced that retail was a good idea since that meant I would be tied up on weekends and someone else would be in charge of my schedule. What were my options? I had been to a home party with Discovery Toys a couple of months prior and I remembered the consultant talking about working from home on a flexible schedule. Perfect! So I called and joined the company and got started. In my first five months, I made enough money with my business for a down payment on our home.

I fell in love with the company, the people and the whole concept of direct sales and continued for 16 years. I worked hard to earn the recognition and rewards, which propelled my business to success. Every year I was one of the top recruiters in the company. Being a top recruiter helped my team grow and soon our organization was amongst the top ranks of the company, with representatives all over the U.S. Building leaders was my focus as I realized there was more to success than my own personal achievement. That strategy proved successful and I was honored to earn the 'Quantum Leap Award' for highest organization growth and I also earned 'Woman of the Year' three times. I achieved Circle of Excellence, was a multiple President's Club achiever every year in sales, recruiting and promoting leaders, became a member of the "Million Dollar Club" and was featured in Success Magazine. Within 3 years of joining my company I left my full time job and made direct sales my career. Joining direct sales was one of the best decisions I have ever made!

Share with us what your business is and why you focus on supporting the direct sales industry?

After so many years in the full time corporate world, joining the direct sales industry really inspired me to find my passion and purpose which is helping others achieve their goals and dreams. Hands-on participation and success in the direct sales industry along with years of coaching and teaching prepared me to offer my experience to direct sellers in quest of success. I truly believe my purpose is to add value to others. This desire and passion for making a difference through helping others resulted in the creation of The Success Factory.

Since I have enjoyed the rewards of being involved in this industry, I know firsthand the struggles people have in trying to build a business. They need the guidance of those who have forged the path, worked a direct sales business themselves and built a large growing team. I have been in the trenches, worked the business and achieved success. I focus on helping others build strong organizations, become dynamic leaders and then teach and train them how to develop leaders.

I work with individuals or companies and can do so in a variety of ways. Coaching and training can be done one on one, in a group setting, or on conference calls or webinars. I am available as an event speaker and I started a leader training retreat, *Get The Advantage Leadership Academy*, that we hold several times a year and is open to anyone in the direct selling industry interested in building a stronger foundation and adding additional layers to their success. It is through these avenues that I can help others improve on the basics of the business; booking, selling, recruiting and team building. I have found that by mastering these basics they become empowered to move into leadership; building organizations that are in growth cycle and building more leaders all the time. Together, we work through the personal challenges so many face in direct sales. Time management, family/business harmony, fear, confidence and belief in themselves. When these things are in sync, not only does their business grow, but their home life thrives. Our mission at The Success Factory is simple; *to help others excel in life, family and business.*

Share your favorite thing about the direct sales industry?

The people! I love the people! People who are attracted to direct sales have incredible entrepreneurial spirits. I love the whole concept of direct sales; it is brilliant! You run your own business yet you have a corporate office that takes care of all the business headaches for you such as, developing and supplying the products and shipping them to your customers. That relieves you of so much responsibility and frees you up to go out and share the products and find others to do the same. On top of that, you are paid - very well – for building your business. As you continue to grow your organization you are rewarded with residual income. That is, money earned for helping others grow their businesses. Marketing experts say that 80% of the cost of getting a product to customers is the result of marketing expenses. Instead of paying loads of money for marketing and advertising, direct sales companies eliminate all the middlemen and pay us for getting the word out about our great products and business opportunity. As technology grows it becomes easier and easier to spread the word. Direct sales is the best!

What is the most rewarding aspect of working with direct sales entrepreneurs?

Direct sellers are a joy to work with and I thrive on listening to their passion and goals for their business. Watching someone grow and develop their skills as their business grows and they begin to blossom into great leaders is so rewarding. No one joins this business thinking, "Oh I am going to have so much personal development!" Yet that is the beauty of direct sales; you personally grow and develop and become better leaders. Helping someone realize their potential and guiding them in the steps to reach it makes my heart sing!

What is your definition of a successful direct sales entrepreneur?

"When the WHY is strong the HOW becomes easy" is my favorite quote from Jim Rohn. To be successful as a direct sales entrepreneur you have to know your "why", your reason, your passion for doing your business. When you are sure of "why" you want to build your business, "how" you are going to do it seems to fall in place because you have a drive and passion for what you are doing. You have to be cemented in your purpose which becomes the heart and soul of why you want to be successful in your business and that will keep you motivated every single day.

What do you consider to be great characteristics of successful entrepreneurs?

Enthusiasm! Positive Outlook. Problem Solver. Drive.
Coachable. Persistent. Good Listener. Generous.

A successful entrepreneur has to be enthusiastic and have a positive outlook and focus on what is right in all situations. You have to be able to get out of the problem and into the solution. Working a consistent business and being persistent are the keys to success in this industry. You have to be tough and not take the no's personally. A crucial trait is that you must be coachable and be willing to put your ego on the shelf and learn. You have to keep growing! Being persistent will help you overcome resistance. You also have to be a good listener and ask good questions to determine how direct sales might be the solution for someone's challenges. Finally, successful entrepreneurs are generous. They understand that their job is to help others. Help others get their fabulous products and join their business and help them be successful.

Zig Ziglar has a quote that I believe sums up our business: *"If you help enough other people get what they want then you will get what you want"*.

Please share what your insights are about the direct selling industry that will best help people build a strong business?

The basics. People forget that this business is the same job over and over again. They get caught up in always looking for new and different ways to do things and forget their job description is simple:

- Love your products
- Share your products with others
- Find others who want to share your products too
- Help them build a team and become a leader.

These are the BASICS of our business and focusing on the basics will ensure you build a growing business.

What advice would you give someone who is ready to take their business to the next level?

The key to taking your business to the next level is developing leaders. You cannot do it all by yourself and your leaders become the legs that hold up your organization. Look for your next leaders. Invite them to be part of your leadership team and let them know you are there to help them every step of the way. Train and coach them on how to build an organization and guide them as they grow and develop their leadership skills.

Basically, what you are doing as you develop leaders is duplicating yourself. When you duplicate yourself by building a leader you are multiplying your efforts. This is when multiplication will take place in your team and in your paycheck!

What is the best description of the relationship between a field member and their corporate office?

What a great question. I watch so many people struggle with this. What I see happen so often is a direct seller starts achieving success and they start being called on by their home office. This makes them feel important. They start giving a lot of their time, usually volunteering, to "help" their corporate office with all kinds of things like training the field, helping with promotions, answering questions, etc. Now, there is nothing wrong with this to a point. I totally believe part of our job is to "give back" to the company that is providing us a business opportunity. However, you have to set boundaries and realize that your JOB is to build YOUR business. Yes, please give some volunteer time to teach a training, speak at convention or train on a conference call. But realize you must focus on your business, your team and revenue producing activities and guard the majority of the time you have to work your business for those things.

I watch so many people want to become great friends with their corporate office and then get their feelings hurt over decisions that are made without asking their advice. Remember they are a BUSINESS, and yes, you are important to them in the field, but they have to be focused on the bottom line and success for the entire company.

The best thing I learned and taught my organization was that the corporate office's job was to provide our products, ship them to our customers and pay us in a timely manner. Our job is to go out and build our business by sharing the products with others and finding others that want to share the products too. Be grateful for the people at corporate and the jobs they do but your focus should be on helping the people on your team. When you have success then be willing to give back by helping but set your boundaries. Your priority is always your personal business and your team.

Consistency and reproducible are terms often used by direct sales leaders. What are some of the most successful systems you have seen used by top leaders?

I see many systems that are great! What I want everyone to realize is that no one ever "organized" their way to the top. Be organized enough to function. Do that by finding a system that works for you and sticking to it.

Make sure that what you do can be duplicated by your team members. This is vital! Always ask yourself, "could a new rep join and do what I am doing?" If you make your job complicated or make it "look" complicated people will not be interested in joining your business. If you make leadership look difficult or like it is too much work, then people will not want to become a leader.

KISS – Keep it Simple Sweetheart! Find a system that works for you. Have fun at your parties! Keep your presentations to under 30 minutes and don't do elaborate set ups. When you do this, your job will look so easy and fun that everyone will want to join! It's not about being perfect – it is about being proactive! Consistency is key – a consistent part time business will succeed!

What are some of the big AH-HAs you have seen entrepreneurs experience that then propel them to the next level?

I will use my own story to answer this question. When I joined direct sales I knew nothing about leadership. At the first event I attended, I received some recognition and wow – I liked it! In my corporate job I was never recognized. When I achieved my quota, the way they recognized me was to give me a bigger quota! Yes, that first time being on stage motivated me to work harder and yes I loved the recognition. I became a great recruiter and that recognition was fun but almost everyone who joined my team quit within a few months. I wanted to be a Director so I set a goal to promote to Director. The key statement in that sentence is that "*I wanted* to be a Director". I tried twice to promote and failed because the focus was on my own recognition and success.

I realized I had no idea how to be a leader. So I started studying everything I could on leadership and reading every book I could find on leadership. I read every book John Maxwell had written on leadership and he opened my mind up to a whole new world. I realized I had been doing what I was taught in the corporate world and trying to "manage" my team members. That doesn't work because in direct sales you are leading a volunteer army. They do not work FOR you they work WITH you and your job is to help them understand and learn how to build and grow a business. It's about what is in it for THEM!

My biggest "ah-ha" was that it was not about ME. I had to take 'Me' and 'I' out of my vocabulary. My job was to help others become successful. It wasn't about ME promoting to Director – it was about US promoting as a Director Team. When I changed those things and talked about THE TEAM more than myself that is when my organization started to explode. It was about me helping others – helping them grow a business and become a leader. When I was focused on helping others promote to leadership our team started growing in amazing ways!

What have direct selling entrepreneurs shared with you that they wish they had known when they started?

How to get over their fear of recruiting and how to be a better recruiter. Selling is obviously a very important part of our business but to build a successful thriving organization you have to recruit. You have to recruit to build a team. You have to recruit to make the great big income.

I will share another personal story to help answer this question. When I first joined direct sales, I spent my first 5 months doing a great job selling. Then I attended a company event where someone congratulated me for my sales and asked me how my recruiting was going. I said "I have no interest in that recruiting thing". She looked at me and said words that truly changed my life. She said "How selfish of you". I was absolutely floored at her comment. Selfish is not a word I would use to describe myself. "What do you mean?" I asked her. She then asked me if I liked the company? Yes. Are you having fun? Yes. Has this business made a difference to your family? Yes, we made enough money in the first five months to make the down payment on a house. And then her words..."Then why would you be selfish and not share it with others?".

WOW – that was the 'ah-ha' moment that changed the course of my business. I had been looking at recruiting as being pushy, trying to convince people or talk them into joining. What I realized was that was not at all what recruiting is about. Recruiting is about sharing our fabulous opportunity with others and letting them know they can be part of it. We are in the sorting business, not the convincing business. We sort through the people we meet, let them know about our business opportunity and then THEY decide if it is a match for their life. We don't "convince" them to join. I don't want to work with anyone I pushed into joining. I want them to be thrilled with their decision to start their own business and be happy to start working!

That day I changed my mindset on recruiting. I went from thinking it was pushy to a mindset of "I have an amazing opportunity that can truly make a difference in someone's life and it is my responsibility to share it". When I changed my mindset then it totally became my heart set; to help people get happily involved with the business because I know this business can be not only income changing but also life changing!

What is a characteristic that you have seen that makes you immediately recognize a future leader?

Truly caring about others. Instead of thinking "what can YOU do to make me successful?" they think "what can I do to make YOU successful?"

Humility. Rick Warren says humility is: *Not that you think less of yourself but you think of yourself less.*

Generosity. A great leader knows their job is to help others. They are "other people" centered and have a heart for helping others achieve their goals and dreams.

What do you see direct sales leaders do to keep motivated and encouraging of their team when things are not going right?

A leader's job is to believe in their team members until they are able to believe in themselves. In the words of Mary Kay, *"Everyone has an invisible sign around their neck that says Make Me Feel Important."*

Recognition is a key factor in motivating and encouraging your team. I truly believe you can never recognize your team members enough. Recognize for everything not just results. Look for reasons to make people feel special. Even simple things like attending the meeting, coming early to help set up the chairs, joining a conference call, making five phone calls or stepping outside of their personal comfort zone. Recognize activity. Activity can be more important than results. If the activity is there, the results will come! Recognize the behaviors you desire. Recognize recruiting! Remember, it is not about the prize or reward. It is the actual act of recognizing someone. Don't spend a lot of money on prizes because it makes being a leader look expensive to those who are your future leaders. Wrapping a candy bar in gold paper can make someone feel special. Present them with a can of Chicken 'N Stars soup. Tell them they used to be "chicken to do things and now they are a star!" Make it fun!

Your job as a leader is to be the coach and the cheerleader. Recognition motivates people to repeat and increase the activity they have been recognized for achieving. Recognize team members at every opportunity and they light up. This may be the first time in their lives they have ever been acknowledged for an achievement. This is powerful! THAT is when you will see that what you are doing is making a difference! Remember your team members will never remember what you gave them but they will ALWAYS remember how you made them feel.

What are the mistakes you have seen leaders make that stifle the growth of their teams?

'Managing' their teams rather than leading them. In direct sales, your team members are not your employees, your job is not to manage them as this can be the quickest way to lose team members. Understand that you are leading a volunteer army. Your job is to teach, train, coach and inspire your team. Realize that every single person who joins your team is different. The beauty and the challenge of a team is that the team is made up of many different personality types. Not everyone may be just like you.

As a leader I had to learn about the different personality styles and become a student of human nature. Once I realized that not everyone was like me – they had different ways of learning, communicating, feeling and being motivated – I was able to work with all styles of people. What I found was there are many people whose fires are there but they might just need a little poking! Learning to work with each person based on their personality style changed everything about my organization. It also helped me attract all kinds of people, not just people like me; after all, that would be boring! It takes all types of personalities to create a successful team! People with different gifts and talents all working together to move forward to success. It is all about understanding each other and learning to respect and celebrate each other's differences. Leaders that do not learn this will have a very difficult time guiding their team. By learning how to work with different personality and learning styles you become a much more effective coach!

What are the biggest surprises/hurdles entrepreneurs face once they become leaders?

Working from home can be the best and worst part of your job. Generally speaking, in the corporate world you have specific duties to perform. You complete them, go home and leave work at the office. In direct sales, you bring a business into your home and you really can never wrap your arms around getting your job "finished". There is always someone else to call, a customer to follow up with, a party to book, a new consultant to train or a leader to coach. What I see happen so often is leaders let their business take over their life. They do not set boundaries. Then they feel guilty when they are working their business that they are not with their family and feel guilty when they are with their family that they are not working their business. It is a vicious cycle that can result in resentment. Even though they love their business they feel stressed and frustrated all the time. Learning to set boundaries with your business and your family is crucial to maintaining the ability to be able to be PRESENT when you are working your business and equally PRESENT when you are with your family. This will result in harmony and you are able to love your business and love your family!

How do successful entrepreneurs create a direct sales business that perpetuates?

Duplication! A good leader is always role modeling what it takes to be successful in this business and teaching it to others. You must be out selling and recruiting to find your next leaders. You have to be in the trenches doing what you are teaching others to do.

Put training systems in place and delegate to future leaders. This teaches them to be a leader. Let others step up and empower them to be leaders! As you build these leaders, you are duplicating your efforts and multiplication continues to take place in your organization. It is as if the train has left the station and is picking up speed. Multiply your team and multiply your earnings.

What is the one key piece of advice you have given to the leaders you coach that has proven the most successful?

Be a servant leader. Truly care and invest in your team members by helping them learn and grow into leadership. Do not see yourself at the TOP of your team. See yourself as the foundation. Your job is to support and nourish your team members to the top as they grow their businesses. You have to have a strong vision for your team and your team members to be able to do big things. A strong vision is nonnegotiable if you want to be successful. Everyone ends up somewhere in life and some people end up somewhere on purpose. Those are the people with vision.

Having a vision and being a servant leader means you believe in your team members before they believe in themselves. Visualize your team growing and visualize each person's success. Create a picture of their success, be excited, and then help them SEE it. I do not think people leave direct sales because they have not had success. I think they leave because they never really caught or visualized their dream and it was not made inspiring enough to keep them motivated.

Remember people buy into the leader before they buy into the vision. That is why you have to be setting the example by working your business, which gives you credibility. You cannot lead your team members beyond where you have gone yourself. Be genuine in caring for others and wanting what is best for them. Let them know you are willing to work to help them achieve their goals.

The highest calling of a leader is to unlock the potential in others. A crucial key to your success will be when you lead as a servant leader with a vision and a belief in others.

What is the best investment you have seen direct sales entrepreneurs make in themselves?

CANI – Constant and Never Ending Improvement. I was taught this early in my business and it has changed my life. A minimum of 15 minutes a day of feeding your mind. Reading books (and I don't mean romance novels!) that can help you with all kinds of things like time management, organization, and leadership. Reaching out for coaching or listening to great trainers who have BEEN THERE and DONE IT. Turn your car into a classroom and listen to podcasts or CDs. Keep a book by your bed and get up 15 minutes early or stay up 15 minutes late and read. Put a book in the bathroom or carry one in your purse; it does not matter how you do it just DO IT!

John Maxwell refers to the Law of the Lid. A leader's organization can never grow higher than the leader's lid. If the leader is a six on a scale of ten as a leader, then their organization can never grow higher than a five. However, if the leader continues to grow as a leader and raises their leadership level to a nine then their team can grow to an eight. A leader has to keep learning and growing to become a better leader. Focus on 15 minutes of CANI a day. Seek out great books, great trainers and great coaches to help you raise your leadership level.

If you were standing in front of 200 new field members who just joined a direct sales company what 3 things would you share?

- Work a part time business not a spare time business. Do at least ONE positive thing every day to move your business forward.
- Share the opportunity. Help people get happily involved! I always say, *"You can survive selling but you will retire by recruiting and you can retire in real style by building a dynamic team"*.
- Discover your WHY and love what you do. Your passion will be contagious.

What have you learned about yourself while working with top leaders in the direct sales industry?

I absolutely LOVE what I do! I love helping others become great leaders. I love helping them build dynamic teams. I love helping people develop a zeal for direct sales and help them build a passion for building leaders. Helping others learn to find harmony with their business and family, learn to dream and dream BIG and become successful is one of the most rewarding things in my life!

How does your expertise help someone building a direct sales business?

I have walked the walk. I have experienced success and failure. I have done things right; but more importantly I have done things wrong and I have learned and grown most from the mistakes I have made. I believe I truly have learned to understand the challenges and frustrations of working with many different types of people. I have successfully built an extremely large organization and developed a lot of leaders and I can help you do the same.

What are the top 3 things you would recommend, based on your expertise, that accelerates business growth?

Learn to be a great recruiter. This business is truly a gift to be shared with others. Once I learned how to effectively share the opportunity with others, this is when my business turned a corner. Become a great leader. Learn how to build a Dynamic Team and promote leaders. When I learned how to do this, my team exploded and we promoted leaders all over the country.

Listen, listen, listen! God gave you one mouth and two ears. Learn to ask good open-ended questions to identify needs, wants and desires in prospective team members and future leaders. Once again the quote from Zig Ziglar is so applicable; *"When you help enough other people get what they want, you will get what you want."*

I have dedicated my life to sharing what I have learned with others. My heart and my passion is truly for helping others be the best person and leader they can be. If someone had told me 24 years ago that direct sales was going to unlock so many treasures in my life; I never would have believed them. Thanks to this amazing industry, I have grown as a woman and an entrepreneur, I have built relationships and made memories that some people only dream of in their life. You can too and I would love to show you how.

Continue the Conversation with Teresa Garrison:

After years in the full time corporate world, joining the direct sales industry inspired Teresa in finding her passion and purpose - helping others achieve their goals and dreams. She focuses on teaching and training others how to develop leaders and build strong organizations. Hands-on participation and success in the direct sales industry along with years of coaching and teaching has prepared her to offer her experience to business leaders in quest of success. She believes her purpose is to add value to others. This desire and passion for making a difference through helping others resulted in the creation of The Success Factory.

Below are the various ways that you can connect with Teresa and learn more about what she has to offer.

- **Website:**
  www.thesuccessfactory.com

- **Facebook:**
  www.facebook.com/thesuccessfactory

49015940R00099

Made in the USA
Lexington, KY
21 January 2016